MONDAY: WHERE I MEET NINJA AND CAVEMAN

Today was a very weird day.

It started when my phone vibrated. I know, my phone vibrating is not weird in itself. It's the reason it vibrated that made it weird. We're not allowed phones in school you see, but you can get away with it as long as they are on silent, and you don't get caught. I keep mine on vibrate. I don't get many messages while I'm at school anyway so it's never been a problem. I've never got caught. Until today.

My phone vibrated and at first I ignored it. Then it vibrated again and again. I was worried that the teacher would notice so I made sure my bag was strategically placed on the table and checked what was going on.

My WhatsApp showed 3 new messages. Now the only person that ever WhatsApp's me is Lisa and she was sat right next to me with her head down pretending to do Maths while actually drawing a tattoo on her arm.

Caveman: Everyone is looking at you

Caveman: Honestly, check it out

Caveman: Oi, listen to me! I'm trying to look out for you

I had no idea who Caveman was. I thought I had my WhatsApp locked down so that weirdos couldn't message me. In fairness, when I first wanted to use WhatsApp, it was the only way my mum would agree to it. And yet, there in front of me were 3 messages from him. I assumed it was a 'him' anyway. I was about to delete the thread and ignore him, when I realised he could now see that I'd read the messages. He would be cross at me for ignoring him. Dammit!

Then the paranoia kicked in. What if he was right? What if he knew something I didn't?

I casually shifted my bag a little and tried to peek around it.

Everyone seemed to have their heads down doing the work the teacher had set. Well, in fairness, Liam was probably the only one actually doing the work. He always did everything he was supposed to. Liam really winds me up. He makes everyone else look bad by getting stuff done. That's just selfish because it makes the rest of us look bad. That's a story for another time though, because while I was grumbling in my head about all the times Liam had made my life more difficult, I hadn't noticed the teacher looking at me.

"Everything ok Emma?"

I swear I nearly jumped out of my skin. Great! If people weren't looking at me before, they definitely were now. They must have thought I was a right idiot. I muttered something about thinking about the maths problem and put my head back down. Lisa stopped drawing on her arm for long enough to give me a 'look'. I shrugged my shoulders and looked at the blank bit of paper in front of me. I was sure everyone now thought I was too stupid to do the work. They had probably all finished ages ago.

The phone vibrated again.

Caveman: Told you so

I nearly picked up the phone and threw it across the room. It was only the fact that Lisa was still looking at me that stopped me. And the amount of trouble I would get in for flinging a phone across the room, of course!

I looked at the maths work. The numbers were all jumbled up and I couldn't make any sense of them. I'm not the best at maths, but I'm normally not the worst either. I glanced over at Lisa's book and noticed she'd finished it all. She was now colouring in the tattoo on her arm with a different coloured pen. It was actually looking pretty good. Lisa had offered to do one for me a few times, but I'd always refused. I said I wanted to do my own. I wasn't going to tell her that my mum would kill me if I came home with something like that on my arm. That would be really sad. We'd been best mates since she moved into the same street as me 3 years ago. Her mother seemed so laid back about stuff like that. She never got any hassle about what she wore. She always had lots of make up on. I once tried to go to school with make up on. My mum caught me and went mental. She made me go upstairs and take it off before I went to school. I wasn't happy. It had taken me ages to get it just right. I'd spent ages watching YouTube videos on how to do it so that Lisa wouldn't tease me. I put it on again when I got to school but it didn't look anywhere near as good. After that I really couldn't be bothered. I just wish she'd give me a break. I wish she was more like Lisa's mother.

The phone vibrated again. I just needed to switch the thing off.

I glanced around. Everyone was doing their own thing.

Caveman: Hurry up and get your work done. They all think you are too stupid to do it.

Me: Shut up! If it wasn't for you I would be doing my work!

Caveman: No need to snap. I'm just trying to help you.

Argh! It was so frustrating.

I took my phone and shoved it in my bag. I needed to get the work done before the bell went. The problem was, no matter how I tried to focus, I just couldn't. My mind kept wandering. What would happen if Lisa got blood poisoning from the tattoo she was drawing on her arm? She was using a Sharpie after all, and my mother had always told me not to draw on myself because I'd get blood poisoning. Were they right?

It was no good. I had to know. I glanced around, then took out my phone again and Googled "Can you get blood poisoning from drawing on your

3

skin?" 1.25 million matches. I guess I wasn't the first to ask that then! (you just Googled it, didn't you?) In case you are wondering, the general idea is that you actually have to swallow a pen to get poisoning from the ink – and even then, you would have to swallow loads of pens to be anything other than a little sick. So, we're safe. I don't think Lisa has any intent to swallow pens.

My phone buzzed.

Dammit, I thought I'd switched it off before I put it back in my bag.

Ninja: It's not true you know.

What the hell? Who was this now? What happened to the Caveman.

Me: It is true. I Googled it.

Ninja: No! not that. It's not true that everyone is going to think you are stupid. Nobody actually cares about you.

I was quite offended by that. At least Caveman seemed to care about me. Ninja was just mean.

Me: That's not very fair. My mum cares about me! And I'm sure Lisa does. We've been best friends for ages.

Ninja: I don't mean that. I mean, if you look around, you'll realise that everyone is too caught up in their own stuff to care what you're up to.

I've got to say, I was quite confused. Besides, how did I end up talking to 2 random strangers on WhatsApp who both claimed to know what I was thinking?

Once more, curiosity got the better of me. I looked around the room. Everyone still had their heads down.

Except Liam. Liam looked at me then looked away again quickly.

Ha! I knew it. Ninja was wrong! Liam was looking at me and thinking I was a total muppet because I couldn't do maths as easily as him. I glared at him. How dare he judge me like that. Creep.

"Emma! You need to do less thinking and more writing otherwise you'll never finish!"

Mr Williams. I hate him. He has it in for me for sure. Everyone else thinks he's great (including him) but I just don't understand a word of what he's saying. It's like he's a Sim speaking that weird Sim language they speak. You think they are speaking a real language until you realise you don't understand a word of what they say. Sometimes I even imagine him with a green diamond above his head! Everyone else is nodding and writing notes and stuff, like what he is saying actually makes sense. And there I am, pretending to make notes but really doodling on my book. He always has a laugh with the lads. They talk about football and rugby and stuff before the class starts. And I noticed Lisa had written his name in a heart on her pencil case. Don't get me wrong, he is good looking, especially compared to the other teachers (Don't get me started on Mr Bentley the Biology teacher!) but that doesn't make him a better teacher in my books.

Every chance he gets he's on my back about something. He never has a go at anyone else. His favourite thing to do is to make me look like an idiot in front of the class. It's like he gets off on it or something.

Just as everyone in the room was staring at me, my phone buzzed again. This time everybody could hear it.

"Was that you?" Mr Williams said, glaring at me "You know you are not allowed phones in school Emma. Bring it here right now."

This was turning into the worst day ever. I slowly took the phone from my bag and walked up to the front of the class with it. I hadn't done anything wrong really, but it totally felt like I was doing a walk of shame. I could almost hear a slow, steady drum beat playing in the background.

I tried not to look at anyone, but caught Liam's eyes as I walked past his desk (which was at the front of the class as usual). He was smiling. Smug creep. Probably thinking it serves me right.

As I reluctantly passed the phone over to Mr Williams, I caught sight of the message that had made it buzz. It was a WhatsApp from Ninja.

Ninja: Don't worry, they really don't care about you

Seriously? I did not need this. I'd lost my phone. The teacher hated me. Everyone in the class thought I was stupid. And to top it all off, I had two total strangers telling me everyone was watching me, and at the same time nobody cared about me. This was a really rubbish day.

I sulked my way back to my desk and slumped down next to Lisa, just as the bell went for end of class. Thank god for that.

I stopped at the teacher's desk on the way past to get my phone back. He refused to look up. Lisa was at the door beckoning me.

"Come on Ems, we'll be late for Biology, and you know what Mr Bentley is like" she whispered urgently.

I rolled my eyes. Yeah, I knew what he was like. But Mr Williams was still refusing to acknowledge my presence and I really wanted my phone back.

"You go ahead" I said, definitely not as a whisper "I will just get my phone and I'll be with you"

Now it was Lisa's turn to roll her eyes. Then, without any loyalty whatsoever she turned and headed off to the next class. I was going to be so late and get in so much trouble. It was all because of Mr Williams – again. He really must hate me.

Once Lisa had disappeared, Mr Williams looked up.

"I'm disappointed in you Emma" he said, holding my phone in his hand and waving it teasingly in my face.

"I know" I muttered. Of course, I knew he was disappointed in me. He hated me.

"You could do so much better if you just knuckled down and worked harder" he continued.

'Yeah' I thought 'if I didn't have a stupid Ninja and a Caveman waffling on at me in WhatsApp while I try and work'.

I said nothing.

He had his ideas about me and nothing I did changed that. In fact, everything I did seemed to make things worse.

A couple of weeks ago we were doing some maths work in class. For once, I totally understood it and managed to finish it ahead of time. Lisa was really struggling so asked me for some help. I was just explaining how I went about it, when Mr Williams shouted at me. He told me that I should let Lisa do her own work and finish mine. I told him I'd already done it, but he said I must have done it wrong because clearly, I did it too quickly. Can't win!

I was aware he was looking at me. Clearly I was supposed to say something but I had no idea what he expected me to say. So, I said nothing but glanced nervously at the doorway.

He sighed and gave me my phone.

"Don't let me catch you on that in my class again" he said.

'Too right. Next time you won't catch me' I thought.

"Thanks" I said, aloud, before turning and quickly walking to my Biology class. We're not allowed to run in the corridors, and I was in enough trouble already.

The rest of the day was pretty uneventful. I kept my phone tucked well away in my bag so as to avoid any further risk of it getting taken off me. I was really glad when the end of day bell rang, and we could make our way to the school bus home.

Lisa and I always rode together on the bus. This was both because we were best friends, and because we lived on the same street so got off at the same stop. Liam was also on the same bus as us. He always sat in the seat in front of us, but as far as I knew, he got off the bus at the stop after ours. He rarely had anyone sat next to him. No one really talked to him. Guess I wasn't the only one to find him creepy.

Today he did something he's never done before. He turned around and looked at me. Lisa and I looked at each other. I don't think either of us knew how to react.

Not only did he look at me, he started talking.

"Sorry about your phone earlier. Mr Williams can be a right idiot sometimes" he said.

Erm, was he being sarcastic? I didn't know him well enough to tell. Liam was the swat swot of the class. I always thought he totally idolised Mr Williams. He certainly always seemed to be sucking up to him. What was he after? What was that look he gave me earlier about?

Just as I was working out what to say back, my phone pinged.

I assumed it was Lisa messaging me to ask what he was on about, as she was on her phone next to me, tapping away.

I looked at my phone. I didn't care that Liam was left hanging there waiting on a response.

Caveman: You're going to die.

What?! What the hell? I needed to block this guy ASAP.

ping

Ninja: Don't listen to him. You're fine. Liam isn't thinking about you. He's just thinking about himself.

I looked up at Liam. He was still staring at me, waiting for an answer.

He really looked like he was thinking about me so I was inclined not to listen to Ninja. Then again, I wasn't particularly big on Caveman's idea that I was going to die. I should probably ignore and block both of them. But who were they? How did they know me? Why were they messaging my phone? How did they even know what was going on. I looked around the bus to see if I could spot some kids that were trying to wind me up. Then I thought it might be Lisa having a laugh at my expense.

I looked over at her. She didn't look up at all. If it was her messaging me as a wind up, surely she would be checking my reaction? Maybe they were messaging her too. She was being awfully secretive and keeping her screen in a position where I couldn't see it.

I shrugged at Liam, "I guess it was my own fault".

Liam looked confused for a second then answered, "I always keep my phone on silent so that doesn't happen to me"

Smug little creep. Lecturing me on what I should do with my phone.

ping

Ninja: He's not lecturing you. He's trying to be helpful.

ping

Caveman: Say something to make him like you. It's important that he likes you. You need to find a mate to survive.

Eww! What was Caveman on about. No way Liam fancied me. And I definitely didn't fancy him!

ping

Ninja: Caveman is right. Liam fancies you.

I looked at Liam. He was pulling at a bit of loose thread on his tatty rucksack. He kept glancing at me and then looking back at the thread.

I'd had enough of this. Everyone was on at me. I took it out on Liam. I actually feel kinda bad about it now. It wasn't really his fault.

"No need to be smug about it" I snapped "You've just basically called me an idiot"

Liam looked like a puppy that had just been kicked. Well, he looked how I imagined a kicked puppy would look. I've obviously never kicked a puppy, or even seen a puppy being kicked!

He pulled at the thread on his rucksack so hard it came off suddenly in his hand, leaving his hand free to fly upwards, smack him in the face and knock his glasses to the floor in the process. Everybody looked at him. Lisa laughed loudly and very obviously.

As I said, looking back I feel quite bad about it.

ping

Ninja: That was just mean. He only wants you to like him. I told you, this is not about you.

I angrily tapped my reply.

Me: What are you on about? He just called me an idiot for getting my phone taken off me. I could tell that's what he was thinking when he gave me that dodgy look in class earlier. You don't know what you are talking about. Leave me alone!

ping

Argh why wouldn't he leave me alone!

Caveman: You need him to like you. It's important. They are all laughing at you.

I felt like throwing the phone out of the window. It was all getting way too much for me. I didn't know what to think anymore.

Before this morning, I had just seen Liam as another kid in the class. Albeit a creepy one. To be avoided at all cost. But now, I wasn't sure.

I messaged Lisa.

Me: Do you think Liam fancies me?

Lisa didn't even bother typing her response. She did one of her snorting laughs and rolled her eyes at me.

I was quite upset by that. Did Lisa think I was that unattractive that not even Liam could fancy me.

ping

What now?

Ninja: Lisa doesn't care.

Oh my god! This guy (I assumed he was a guy too) was driving me up the wall.

I looked at my phone and checked my bag and my clothes. He must have a video camera or something near me. I couldn't find anything, but that didn't mean it wasn't there.

Lisa was frantically tapping away on her phone again. I expected my phone to ping with a message from her, but nothing came through.

I looked over to see who she was typing to, but she hid the screen from me again. I bet she was messaging someone about me. This day was turning out to be a total disaster.

Liam, meanwhile, had managed to pick up his glasses from the floor and was now picking away at a different thread on his rucksack. The only difference now was that his face was bright red.

Everyone else on the bus had gone back to their conversations.

I stared at my phone.

I didn't know what to do. I didn't know what to think.

Lisa was now looking at her phone and giggling away to herself. I could see that she was on Facebook. Weird, I didn't have any new message notifications. Neither of us went onto Facebook much anymore so it struck me as strange that she had it open. I opened Facebook on my phone, and there in front of me was a picture of Liam punching himself in the face. Someone must have caught it on camera and shared it. I smiled. He looked like a right muppet. Then, as I studied the photo more I realised something else. Off to the side in the picture you could see me, and I was pulling the weirdest face! How embarrassing. Oh my god, everyone must have been looking at it and thinking I looked like a right muppet. I started to panic. My heart was beating so loudly at this stage that everyone on the bus must have been able to hear it.

Then, I realised, from the angle of the photo, that Lisa had taken the picture! Lisa had taken the picture and shared it with everyone but not tagged me, so I wouldn't realise. She was laughing at me. Everyone was laughing at me.

ping

Caveman: You should have listened to me. Now we're doomed.

For once, I was inclined to agree with Caveman. I actually started feeling sorry for Liam. I could feel everyone on the bus looking at me and laughing. What hurt most was that Lisa was one of them. I thought she was my friend. I thought of saying something to her but then decided against it. What was the point? She'd just laugh at me after all.

It was going to be all over Facebook by the evening and so by tomorrow the whole school would be talking about it.

I started feeling sick. Maybe it was just the motion of the bus as it bumped around the back streets, or maybe it was something else but I really felt like I was going to barf. That really would seal the deal if I went and barfed on the bus. I looked up and tried to look through the front window of the bus. This always worked for me when I was younger and got terribly travel sick. My mother had taught me to look out of the front window and count to 10, exhaling and blowing raspberries in between each number. I obviously wasn't going to do the raspberry thing, but I could at least look up and breathe.

The problem was, I could now see everyone looking at their phones and looking over at me. What should I do? Look forward and feel like an idiot, or look down and risk barfing.

Funnily enough, it was Liam who saved me.

"Ignore them" he said "that's what I do. They'll have forgotten about it by tomorrow and be on to something else. Probably something else I have done" he said, and then stared out of the window for a few seconds. I was sure I could see tears in the corner of his eyes.

Lisa sniggered next to me.

I shoved my elbow in her side.

"Oi!" she yelled "that hurt!"

"Oh, really sorry" I said, pretending to sound genuine "the bus just swerved and I was just trying to stop myself falling over"

Lisa rolled her eyes and went back to checking her phone, smiling to herself occasionally.

ping

Ninja: Told you.

What? What did he tell me? That no one cared? Clearly, he was wrong. Clearly the whole school cared. Actually, maybe he was right about one person. Lisa. Lisa obviously wasn't the friend I thought she was. If she'd cared about me she wouldn't have shared that photo on Facebook. I began to wonder what else she was up to behind my back.

I leant over to Liam.

"Have you seen the photo on Facebook? It's so embarrassing."

"I don't have Facebook" he said.

"What?!" I said, a little louder that I planned. Then again, everyone was already looking at me so I guess giving them yet another reason didn't really matter. How could anyone not have Facebook? Maybe he was just like the rest of us and had fallen out with Facebook but was now on Snapchat.

"So, Snapchat? WhatsApp"

"Nope" he said.

"Anything?"

He just shook his head.

"Do you even have a phone?"

He shook his head again.

Wow, a 15-year-old without a phone. He must be the only one in the world.

"So, what do you do then? How do you talk to your friends?" I thought maybe he was using something I hadn't heard of yet. After all, everyone knew he was a geek.

He just shrugged his shoulders and muttered "I don't have any friends, so it doesn't matter"

Once more I found myself at a loss for words. How could he not have any friends?

"You must have at least one friend?" I asked.

He shrugged again.

"No one likes me" he said, in a slightly defensive and pathetic tone.

I didn't mean it to sound like it did. I genuinely couldn't believe that someone would have no friends at all. My mother always told me there was somebody out there for everybody. Usually when I was moaning about Lisa going out with her boyfriend again and leaving me at home all on my own. I obviously didn't talk to my mother about that sort of stuff most of the time.

So, there I was, having had the most rubbish of rubbish days at school, sat on the school bus with my supposed best friend making fun of me on Facebook on one side, everyone else on the bus laughing at me. Bizarrely, I find the only person I now had anything in common with was Liam, the class creep.

Meanwhile I had a Caveman and a Ninja reading my mind, watching my every move, and being all judgemental of everything I was doing. The phrase 'between a rock and a hard place' came to mind.

Just then the bus lurched to a stop and Lisa began shoving me.

"Come on" she huffed impatiently "shift. This is our stop"

A moment ago I had been desperate to get off the bus, but now it was my stop, my legs felt like lead. I was dreading walking past everyone. I let Lisa shove her way past me, barely glancing up from her phone.

Then, I was surprised to see Liam get up. It wasn't even his stop. He started walking then glanced back at me. He gestured with his head for me to follow him. Everyone was looking at him. Some were pretending not to.

Others didn't care and were just laughing in his face. I've got to say, I was impressed. He just kept walking. And I followed. Knowing everyone was looking at him and not me.

When we got off the bus, there was no sign of Lisa.

"Ignore her" said Liam.

Geez, could everyone read my mind these days?

I just shrugged. It seemed a bit weird to be getting advice on something like this from the class creep who admitted he didn't even have any friends.

ping

Liam gave me a look. The look said, 'don't look at your phone'. He didn't understand what it was like. He had no friends. He didn't know how the curiosity about who a message was from could eat away at you and you were properly at risk of losing your mind if you didn't check.

It was taking all my willpower not to look. Maybe it was Lisa. Maybe she was apologising for being a pig.

ping

That was it. One message I could just about manage to ignore, but two messages would kill me.

Ninja: You know he can't read your mind, right? He's just guessing because that's what he is thinking and he assumes you are the same. And Lisa is just trying to look cool and clever by making you look stupid. It really is all about her.

The second message was from Caveman.

Caveman: Wow that was a close one. You have some real damage limitation to do now. You really need to make up with Lisa. She's your best friend and you don't want her upset with you. Oh, and make sure that you keep Liam as a friend too. You might need him. After all, you haven't got a boyfriend and you need a boyfriend if you are going to fit in.

I supposed Ninja could be right about Lisa. She was always quick to make fun of everyone else. She was worse when she was with her boyfriend. It's one of the reasons I didn't hang out with her when she was with him. All they would do was bitch about everyone else. I usually laughed and went along with them, but it made me feel quite uncomfortable.

ping

Ninja: You know, if she's saying that stuff about everyone else when she's with you, what do you think she says about you when she's with others?

I turned to Liam. He was slowly walking along in the direction of my house.

"You don't like Lisa much, do you?"

"I couldn't care less about her" he shrugged "I know she's your best friend and all, but I don't think she treats you very well. She doesn't seem to treat anyone well to be honest" and then he resumed walking slowly with his eyes firmly planted on the path in front of him.

I always felt quite lucky to be friends with Lisa. She was definitely one of the more popular girls in the school. Not the sort of person that would be friends with me normally. I assumed it was because we liked the same stuff that we ended up friends, but when I thought about it, we didn't. She was always making fun of my taste in music. So much so, I had started to pretend to like the same stuff as her. Whenever I asked her if she was free to hang out, she told me she was busy with something else, or that her mum wouldn't let her. Yet, whenever there was homework to be done, she was always asking to come round to mine.

I tried to remember a time where she had said anything good about anybody, and I couldn't. Maybe Ninja was right? I looked at Liam again. He was shuffling along close to me. I was pretty sure he lived quite a bit away from me because he had never got off at this bus stop before. And yet, today he'd got off at this stop with me and now appeared to be walking me home. Why? Why would he do that? Up until this afternoon, I'd never had any sort of conversation with him. In fact, I'd only ever glared at him and called him a creep.

I'd known Liam for way longer than I'd known Lisa. He was in the same primary school as me. I couldn't remember much about him from back then. He had always seemed like a nice enough kid.

I stopped in my tracks. Liam didn't notice. He just carried on shuffling along, so I was able to just look at him. I looked at him properly, for the first time in a long time. His head was down. His rucksack was as scruffy as the rest of his clothes. He looked like he was trying to be invisible. It was like I was seeing him for the first time. When had I started thinking of him as a creep? And then I heard Lisa's voice in my head:

"Look at that *boy* over there" she said with real disdain as we were walking around the school one lunch break. "He's such a creep. He doesn't ever look at anyone. He just glances at them all creepy and sneaky like"

I looked across and saw that she was talking about Liam.

"Oh, he's harmless" I had stupidly said "I was at primary school with him. He's nice enough"

Lisa had given me one of her special 'looks'.

"Seriously Ems. You are gonna get in so much trouble. You are a rubbish judge of character. He is obviously a total creep"

I couldn't see what she meant, but as I'd only recently become friends with her I didn't want to upset her by disagreeing with her. So instead I laughed nervously

"Yeah, I guess you're right. I just never noticed before" and then for good measure I added "creep".

Lisa had seemed satisfied that I had been educated, and had returned to talking about what she did with her boyfriend the night before. She always over-shared what they had got up to. It usually started with "I know this is TMI but…" and then she went on to share all the details. I didn't want to know, but I didn't feel I could tell her that. I tried once and she just laughed and ignored me.

When I thought about it, Lisa never said anything good about anyone. I wondered what she said about me when I wasn't around.

Liam had noticed that I was no longer walking with him. He stopped and looked over at me. Clearly noticing a weird look on my face, he asked:

"Are you ok? Did I do something wrong?"

I laughed. Why on earth would he think he'd done something wrong? All he was doing was walking!

And there it was again; the look on his face like I'd just kicked a puppy.

ping

I looked at my phone. I had no idea why Liam was getting so upset.

Ninja: I told you, no one can read your mind. He has no idea what you are thinking. He is too busy being caught up in his own thoughts to know what you are thinking.

ping

Caveman: You should go after Lisa. And will you stop being mean to Liam. You really, really need to fit in. I can't stress how important it is

ping

Ninja: Don't listen to Caveman. He's wrong. He's still thinks you're in the caveman days and that a pack is critical to survival. You don't need to fit in. You are perfectly ok just being you.

ping

Caveman: What? Ninja is gonna get you killed. You have *got* to listen to me. It's really, really, really important. Go after Lisa right now and tell her you're sorry.

I flicked the switch on my phone to put it on silent, and shoved it into the pocket of my bag. I'd had enough of these two. They really weren't helping.

"Why on earth would you think you'd done something wrong?" I asked Liam "You haven't done anything other than help me with that stupid stuff on the bus"

He just shrugged again.

"I dunno" he muttered "seems to be the only thing I'm any good at, messing things up for people".

I was genuinely surprised. Liam was good at everything. Well, except for sports and socialising. But everything else. He was top of the class in all subjects at school. The teachers seemed to think the sun shone out of his a**e. Why would he think that he was rubbish at everything?

"Seriously?" I said, easily catching up with him again. "I wish I was as rubbish at everything as you. Teachers all think you're great and you seem to find all the subjects at school easy. You don't have to worry about the grades you're going to get in your exams, like I do!"

"Yeah, but none of that matters when nobody likes you" he replied, "I'd rather be stupid and popular"

I waited for him to say 'like you', but he didn't. He just returned to looking at the ground.

"This is your house, isn't it?" he asked.

How did he know where I lived?

"Erm…yeah" I said. And then there was this weird awkward silence.

"Want to come in?" I asked.

I have no idea why I asked him that. Maybe it was because I felt sorry for him, standing there all scruffy and insecure. Maybe it was because I felt guilty over thinking he was a creep. Or maybe it was because I was genuinely grateful for his help.

He looked shocked, and was just about to answer when I heard Lisa yell from across the road:

"Hey Ems! I'll be over in five to do that homework yeah?"

Seriously? She was acting like nothing had happened. Part of me was quite glad though. It meant that she wasn't upset with me and that we were still friends. Caveman's words echoed in my head, 'You really, really need to fit in'.

"Erm…" I really wasn't sure what to say. Should I stay mad at her? Was I letting her know everything was ok if I let her come over. Before I had time to work out what I wanted to do she yelled:

"Great! See you in 5!" and then disappeared back into her house.

I turned around to let Liam know that he was still welcome to come in, but he'd gone. I looked around in time to see his rucksack disappearing round the corner at the end of the road. Ah well, I guess he wasn't up for coming in.

Lisa knocked on the door about half an hour later (she was always late) and, as usual, she spent most of the time going on and on about all the different people we knew (and some I didn't) and all the things they did that she didn't approve of. She also, as usual, went on and on about what she had done with her boyfriend over the weekend. We got very little homework done. Neither of us mentioned what had happened on the bus.

So yeah, that was a very strange day. I gotta admit, I am dreading tomorrow. Even though things seem cool with Lisa, I'm not sure I want to go on the bus in the morning and have everyone looking at me.

TUESDAY: THE MORNING AFTER THE NIGHT BEFORE

I really didn't want to go to school today. I woke up this morning feeling like I was going to be sick. Mum is at college right now and so sometimes she is out of the house before me, but sometimes she doesn't go in at all. I had really hoped that this was one of her college days. Unfortunately, it wasn't.

"Ems, you're going to be late for the bus!" she yelled up the stairs.

I buried my head under the pillow. If I was quiet, maybe she'd think I'd already gone.

It didn't work. A few seconds later there was a banging on the door of my room and my mum just walked in. I really wish she wouldn't do that. It's my room and it's an invasion of privacy.

"Muuuum get out!" I yelled. Admittedly, this was not the most sensible course of action to get my mother to leave me alone. But, in my defence, I was feeling rubbish and wasn't really thinking straight.

Needless to say, that didn't go down well with my mum.

"Enough already Ems, you have to get to school. This is a big week for you. You've got your exams coming up"

I moaned. This is what it always came down to. Exams. I am so rubbish at xams! My whole life is going to be ruined because I can't remember how to add up x's and y's. Like I'll ever need to do that in real life. Every single class, all the teachers go on about how important these exams are for the rest of my life. I have no idea what I want to do next week, let alone for the rest of my life. I kind of fancy doing something with Psychology, but I can't stand Mrs Knight, the Psychology teacher, so there is no way I'm doing that class.

"You won't be able to do this when you're older you know? If every time something gets a little difficult you decide to take the day off sick, you'll never be able to keep a job."

I had stopped listening at this point. I knew what came next. She would tell me about how she'd had to give up college to have kids and how she regretted it all the time because all her friends had gone on to have amazing jobs, while she was just left behind struggling for money and bringing up a kid.

I'd lost count of how many times I'd heard that story. I don't know why she needed to keep reminding me that she didn't want me in her life. How on earth was that supposed to encourage me?

Besides, she had no clue. She thought I was avoiding going into school because of exams. It wasn't that. I was really feeling ill. It wasn't the thought of the exams making me feel worse, it was the thought of catching the bus. Everyone was going to be looking at me. That picture from Facebook kept flashing into my head. It made me cringe so much.

"I know you don't believe me" I moaned "but my stomach really hurts"

"I believe you" she answered "I know your stomach is sore. What I don't believe is that you are ill. I think your stomach is just telling you that you're stressed"

I hated it when she said something that was impossible to argue with, so instead of even trying to argue, I let out a frustrated growl and buried my head under the pillow again.

I thought it had worked because she didn't say anything else. I snuck a peek from under my pillow, half expecting to see her standing there quietly with her arms folded, but she was gone. Result! Emma =1, Mother = 0.

Then, without the pillow muffling my hearing, I could hear her talking to someone downstairs. At first I thought maybe Lisa had called round for me. She'd never done that before, but maybe she was feeling guilty about yesterday? Then I realised that it was a male voice. Who on earth could be here at this time in the morning?

Curiosity got the better of me, and I quickly threw on my school uniform, brushed my hair, and applied a sneaky bit of makeup. Not enough so that my mum would notice, unless she looked closely, but enough that Lisa wouldn't go on at me again about my spotty face putting her off her food.

I looked over the bannister at the top of the stairs to see who was there, and was surprised to see that the front door was closed. Whoever it was, they had either gone away or my mother had invited them in the house. Probably the former. We didn't really know anyone. I crept downstairs quietly, avoiding the creaky stairs, and peeked around the corner into the lounge.

Sitting on the sofa with their back to me, was the person whose voice I could hear. My mother was standing up chatting to them. She caught site sight of me and smiled. In her 'visitor' voice she said:

"Your friend here came to see if you were going to school this morning. Isn't that nice of him?"

I rolled my eyes. I knew exactly what she was thinking. By now, I had worked out that this was Liam. I was quite used to seeing the back of his head as I always sat behind him on the bus and in class. Also, the tatty rucksack by the side of the sofa was a total giveaway. Now my mother thought Liam was my boyfriend and I was never gonna hear the end of it!

"She's had a bit of a dodgy tummy this morning and wasn't sure if she was going in" she continued, talking to Liam.

"Muuum!" I was mortified. Why was she telling this to a total stranger? In fact, why had she invited him into the house in the first place? As if today wasn't going to be bad enough already, she'd now totally embarrassed me in front of Liam too. I couldn't see Liam's face, but I was pretty sure he would be laughing at me.

I grabbed my school bag and headed for the door, before it was too late and I literally died of embarrassment.

"Wait up!" my mother shouted after me "You've not had your breakfast yet. You should get something to settle your tummy"

There she went again. She was always on at me to eat. Eat your breakfast. Make sure you have a good lunch. Eat all your dinner.

"I'm not a kid mum" I snapped. "I'm not hungry. I'll get something at school". This was a lie. I had no intention of eating breakfast. I hadn't eaten breakfast for weeks. Not since Lisa pointed out my fat thighs when we did gym.

I couldn't get out the door quick enough. So much so, that I almost forgot about Liam sitting there on the sofa. I stopped short of slamming the door and glared at him.

"You coming or what?" I asked curtly.

Liam glanced round, and stumbling awkwardly, half ran, half skipped out of the living room and out of the door, tripping over the doorstep as he went. He muttered something and followed as I walked as fast as I could, without actually breaking into a run, away from the house.

When he caught up with me, he said nothing. He just walked alongside me until we reached the bus stop.

I was fuming. How dare he just turn up at my house like that. Now everyone was going to think we had something going on. I would never hear the end of it from my mother. And to make it worse, there I was, on my way to school, when I had no plans to go in today, or maybe ever again. Damn my curiosity for making me go downstairs to see who was there.

I felt relieved when I noticed Lisa wasn't at the bus stop. Although in fairness, she was never there before me. She always came dashing out of her house last minute and was pretty much the last person on the bus. I once assumed she wasn't going to come in that day, and sat next to someone different on the bus. She jumped on the bus just as the doors were closing, and when she realised I hadn't kept her a seat, really laid into me. So much so, I ended up standing up and letting her have my seat. That meant I had to stand up for the rest of the journey to school. I nearly fell over loads of times because I was standing in the middle of the bus with just the upright bar to hold onto. Every time I put my hand up too high, Lisa had prodded me in the middle and said "Eurgh, get your stinky pits outta my face!" I had put deodorant on that morning too! Mind you, I made a point of changing it after that and making sure I always had plenty of the stuff on before I left the house.

Except for this morning. This morning I had totally forgotten to put deodorant on. Dammit. I moved my arms in a bit closer to my body so that nobody would get a whiff. That would be the icing on the cake to have everyone laugh at me and call me smelly.

ping

My first thought was that Lisa must be messaging me to tell me she was running late. I scrabbled around in my bag for my phone and at first panicked that I'd forgotten to bring it. Then I had a 'duh' moment where I realised that I wouldn't have heard it ping unless it was in my bag! Anyway, it turned out it was one of those nutters on WhatsApp again (why hadn't I blocked them?)

Caveman: Say something to Liam. You need to talk to him. You've got a lot to fix after yesterday if you are going to be ok. Talk to him. Make him like you. It's important that he likes you.

I looked over at Liam, who was now slumped against a wall, staring at the floor. Caveman had a point. I needed all the friends I could get right now. I had a quick look around for Lisa and then went and leant against the wall next to him.

"How come you're at this stop today?" I asked.

He shrugged (I was getting used to that shrug of his now).

"I guess I figured you could use some company after yesterday on the bus. No big deal, I don't live that far away" he said.

"That's really sweet of you" I said. I was genuinely surprised. "but why would you do that for me? We've not exactly been best friends"

He shrugged again.

"Dunno. Guess I just know what it's like."

I began to feel sorry for Liam. I just thought he kept himself to himself because he didn't like any of us, or, thought he was better than everyone else. I hadn't, for one moment, considered that it might not be his choice. But why was he being nice to me after everything I'd said (and thought!) about him.

ping

Ninja: He doesn't know what you think of him. He can't read minds. No one can. And he doesn't know what you have said about him behind his back because...well...erm...it was behind his back!

Now I felt guilty. If Liam knew what I'd been saying about him, would he be so nice to me? I doubted it.

Up until then, I hadn't really engaged with either Caveman or Ninja, but now I felt I needed a bit more help. I was beginning to realise that the way I had seen things up until then was not necessarily the only way of seeing them. I was questioning everything about myself and everyone around me. And I was feeling pretty bad about the way I'd treated Liam, and quite annoyed at Lisa for the way she was treating me.

Just when I was about to reply, Liam gave me a nudge pointed at the school bus that had just arrived. I shoved my phone in my bag and was about to get on the bus in front of him, when he put his arm across me.

"Let me go on first" he said, "that way all the focus is on me and they might forget about you"

"You sure?" I asked. I really had misjudged this guy.

"Yeah. As I said, I'm used to it" and with that he stepped onto the bus and shuffled along to his usual seat near the front. As I looked around, I spotted at least 5 of the other people on the bus pointing at the phone and looking over at him and grinning.

Then I realised that, nice though the idea was, his plan had a fundamental flaw in it. He was now in his seat, and I had to walk the full length of the bus if I was going to sit where I usually sat with Lisa. There was no longer anyone else for them all to focus on than me. Of course, I could always go and sit next to Liam, who was looking at me. Oh god, whatever I did it was going to be wrong. I either sat with Liam and kept him happy but ended up with everyone talking about me, or I ran the gauntlet of the whole bus to the back seats and tried to ignore the sniggering and pointing.

I was frozen to the spot. I had no idea what the best way through this was. This was exactly why I didn't want to go to school today.

Then I felt a shove in my back.

"Come on Ems, shift your butt!".

Lisa had done her usual and jumped on the bus last minute as the doors were closing. Now she was making the decision for me. There was no way I could go and sit with Liam now that Lisa was there.

"Ow!" I grumped "go on then if you're in such a rush"

Lisa shoved me out of the way and strode along to the back of the bus . I glanced at Liam to try and give him an apologetic look, but he had turned away from me and was looking out of the bus window. Well, he was pretending to look. The windows were filthy as usual. I slunk along behind, doing my Liam impression and staring at the ground to avoid making eye contact with anyone. The bus made me move a little quicker than planned, as it set off from the bus stop jerking me forward so I landed in the seat next to Lisa with a thump. She laughed at me and started tapping away on her phone.

I wondered what she was writing. Was she making fun of me again? Was she sharing something on Facebook?

As the bus bumped and swerved along the road to school, I took out my phone and started talking to Ninja.

Me: So how do you know what I'm thinking if you go on about not being able to read minds?

Ninja: I don't know what you are thinking. I can just guess because I know how people generally think.

Ninja: …and I care about you

That was a little weird. But I wanted to hear more, so I decided to let that last comment slide.

Me: Ok, so what is Lisa thinking right now?

Ninja: No idea.

Me: Oh come on! You've been pestering me since yesterday and now I decide to actually talk to you, you shut up?

Ninja: Seriously, I have no idea what she's thinking. Neither do you. That's the whole point. If I had to guess, I would say she is trying to make herself more popular by making fun of someone else. Lisa is very insecure.

Clearly Ninja had no idea what he was talking about. Lisa was the most confident person I had ever met. There wasn't even a hint of insecurity about the way she acted. I was beginning to regret engaging with Ninja. Obviously I had been right, he was a nutter! I decided to change the subject.

Me: What's the deal with this Caveman guy? Do you know him?

It took a moment for Ninja to respond.

Ninja: He's like me in many ways. He really cares about you and wants to make sure you are safe. The problem is, the things he thinks are going to hurt you, are the things that hurt him in his childhood.

I knew not everyone was as lucky as me. When I was younger we had passed a homeless guy outside the shop we were just about to go into. He was wearing scruffy clothes, and stank. When he spoke, he slurred his words and his eyes half closed. To be honest, he scared me. I held onto my mother's hand a little tighter and asked, in what was probably a way too loud voice: "Why is that man asking for money? Why doesn't he just go and get a job?". My mother had shooed me inside and then explained how some people have such horrible lives at home that it is better to live on a pavement than it is to be at home. Other people find themselves in a place where they don't have enough money to pay for somewhere to stay. We bought him a sandwich from the shop and I gave it to him when we left. Since then, I have always given money, clothes or food to homeless people whenever I have passed them.

Me: Oh, I'm sorry to hear that. That's rubbish. But surely he knows that I've had a pretty good childhood?

Ninja: Oh no, you misunderstand me. He didn't have a rubbish childhood. He's a caveman. Everything was risky for him and could potentially kill him. He just thinks the same is true for you. So, if you get hurt by someone saying something mean, he thinks that's as bad as getting hurt by a sabre-toothed tiger and tries to protect you. He's been doing it your whole life, it's just you didn't realise.

Me: Wait…you're saying you guys have always been around? Where are you? Why are you here? And why haven't I heard from you before?

Ninja: Geez, has anyone ever told you that you ask way too many questions? It's kind of hard to explain where we are. But we are here to look after you. It's just that often (all the time in fact!) Caveman and I have differences of opinion on what looking after you actually means. Then yesterday, I was having a row with Caveman about what was going on in class, and suddenly you could hear that on your phone. Or see it. Or whatever. But anyway, you started responding. Which was weird and freaked us both out to be honest.

Me: It freaked you out! What about me? I've two weirdos messaging me on WhatsApp all of a sudden and getting me in trouble with the teacher. I'm not really clear how you call that looking out for me. You just caused me all sorts of problems!

Just then the bus lurched to a stop, making me drop my phone into Lisa's lap. It appeared we had arrived at school and my chat was over. Lisa picked up my phone, looking at it as she passed it back to me.

"Who you talking to?" she asked as I grabbed the phone off her before she could read any of the conversation.

"No one really" I shrugged and, shoving my phone in my bag, I strode off down the bus before she could ask any more questions. I was so busy trying to get away, that I walked right into Liam as he was getting out of his seat.

"Watch it!" I snapped, not realising it was him. There it was again, that hurt puppy look.

"Oh, sorry Liam, I didn't realise it was…ow!" Lisa shoved right past me pushing me on to Liam and knocking him back into his seat with me on top of him. I was mortified but clearly not as bad as Liam was. I could practically feel the heat from his bright red face. I awkwardly pushed myself off him, trying hard not to put my hands anywhere too personal. He just lay there like an upside-down tortoise, equally trying not to touch me anywhere, with his face glowing with embarrassment.

"What the hell!" I yelled at Lisa when I got myself upright again.

She just stood there laughing. She wasn't the only one either. Everyone on the bus seemed to find it very funny, including the driver. Everyone except me, that is. And everyone except Liam.

I really, really should have stayed at home today!

I pushed past Lisa and got off the bus as quickly as I could. I was fighting tears. My life was over. All I wanted to do was run out of the school gates. I started seriously thinking about how I could leave school right there and then without anyone noticing. Problem was, it was the week before my exams and I lived too far away to walk. And I had no money. All of that meant I would not only have to get through the whole school day, but I would also have to go home on the bus.

I seriously had no idea how I was going to do that.

"Hey Ems, wait for me" yelled Lisa who had obviously managed to stop laughing for long enough to get off the bus.

I stopped and fought hard to compose myself. It didn't matter. Lisa didn't even look at me. She didn't seem to have any idea how upset I was. She just hooked her arm through mine and walked me into school, chattering away obliviously. That put paid to any sort of escape plan I had. It looked like I was just going to have to get through the day somehow.

"Double maths today eh?" she sighed. "Although Mr Williams does make it easier, don't you think?"

She didn't even wait for an answer. She just carried on talking.

"I mean, I'm not a big fan of maths, as you know. But I reckon I'll do ok in my maths exam with your help. It will just be a bit of a shame when Mr Williams isn't our teacher any more, don't you think?"

We'd spoken about Mr. Williams quite a lot. I'd told Lisa how he had it in for me. She never seemed to listen though. No matter what I said, she still thought he was great, because he was good looking. I always dreaded maths, and yesterday's interaction had just made me dread it more.

I decided that the only way to get through the day would be to knuckle down and get on with my work. I would ignore everything Lisa said or did, and not let it affect me. It was going to be a bit trickier with the teachers, but maybe, if I just worked hard, they would see that I was trying and give me a bit of a break.

My strategy worked for most of the day. This was probably helped by the fact that I didn't have any lessons with Liam for the first part of the day, and I had my favourite subject; Art. Neither Lisa nor Liam had taken Art as a subject, so I had the class all to myself. For me, the Art class was my safe place. It felt like the only place I could truly be me. The teacher, Mrs Wilson, seemed to really get me. We could talk about materials, and styles and favourite artists for almost the whole lesson. She even had a kettle in her room so her students could drink tea and coffee while painting. It was a blissful hour; a little oasis in the middle of the day. Luckily, the lesson was just before lunch, so today I asked if I could stay in through my lunch break.

We weren't normally allowed to stay in school during breaks, unless it was absolutely bucketing it down outside. Today was a clear dull day. I think Mrs Wilson sensed that something was wrong and said that it was fine, but she had to go to the staff room so I'd have to be on my own. This suited me down to the ground, as I didn't actually plan on eating anything for lunch, despite the fact that my stomach was rumbling loudly. Eating wasn't going to get rid of my fat thighs. I'd had more than enough of being laughed at over the last couple of days. I couldn't control some of that other stuff, but I could definitely control the way I looked. To seal the deal, I offered to wash all the brushes in preparation for her next lesson.

The bell rang for lunch and everyone grabbed their bags and headed out of the door. Mrs Wilson made one final check that I would be ok, then headed out the door herself.

Silence. A most wonderful experience. Well, at the start of lunch break at least. After about 10 minutes it was pretty lonely actually. I realised I'd forgotten to put my phone on silent with all the drama on the bus, and as my next lesson was maths, I needed to fully silence it otherwise I would have it taken off me again. Luckily, I'd not had any messages all morning. I figured I would check what was going on and maybe, if I could pluck up the courage, check out the comments on my photo on Facebook from yesterday. I reached into my bag, but my phone wasn't in the pocket I normally put it in. Deciding I must have shoved it in the wrong place, I searched all through my bag. No joy. I was beginning to panic. I couldn't find my phone. What would I do without my phone? Apart from anything else, Lisa could have posted anything about me and I'd have no clue. I wasn't as worried about the two nutters on WhatsApp as I was about keeping up with what was being said about me.

Where could I have lost it? I worked back in my mind through the whole day. My heart sank when I realised that the only place I could have lost it was on the bus, when Lisa shoved me onto Liam. It must have fallen out of my bag then.

My mum was going to kill me. She gave me a massive lecture when she gave me that phone about how it was expensive technology and I needed to be responsible and not lose it or break it because she wouldn't be getting me another. The annoying thing was I had been careful. I'd even bought a special case for it with my own money. And now I'd lost it. Could this day get any worse?

I spent the rest of the lunch break freaking out and trying to work out whether it was going to be better telling my mum outright, or whether I should keep it secret from her. My stomach rumbled annoyingly. It made it hard to think. I was finding it really hard to focus on anything. I wished it would just shut up. I decided to make a cup of tea. That should shut up my stomach. I made the tea, but there was no milk. I really couldn't drink tea without milk, so I poured it away again. I filled the cup with water. Problem was, the cup was still hot after the tea, so now I had warm water. I poured that away too and gave up. I focussed on cleaning brushes and tables. At least that didn't require much focus.

After lunch it was double maths. Having managed to avoid them all day, I was now in a classroom with Lisa and Liam again.

"Where were you at lunch?" Lisa asked. "I tried to message you but you were ignoring me. You upset with me or something?"

'No Lisa' I thought. 'Why on earth would you think I was upset with you? You took a ridiculous picture of me and shared it with everyone without telling me, shoved me multiple times and made me lose the very phone that you were trying to message me on!'

She really was clueless. However, out loud I said:

"I was in art class. I had stuff to do for Mrs Wilson. And I left my phone at home today" That was a lie but I didn't want to tell Lisa that I'd lost my phone. I didn't trust her not to accidentally-on purpose tell my mum next time she was round.

"No you didn't" she replied. "You had it on the bus this morning. You were messaging some weirdo called Ninja"

Dammit. I'd forgotten that. And quite clearly she had done more than glance at my phone when I passed it over.

Found out. I needed to recover from this.

"Doh! What am I like?" I laughed "I had it on silent and assumed I'd left it at home. I totally forgot about this morning". Another lie. This was becoming quite a habit for me these days.

Lisa rolled her eyes at me again.

We walked through the classroom to the desk at the back of the room where we always sat, chucked our bags on the table and chatted a bit while we waited for everyone else to arrive and settle.

"Right, settle down everyone" It was an unfamiliar voice, commanding us from the front of the room. I clearly was not the only one surprised into silence, as the rest of the room also went quiet.

There was a woman stood at the front of the class. She didn't really look like a teacher. She was wearing jeans and a plain black shirt. I couldn't, if you had asked, describe what a teacher should look like. But I could tell you that this woman didn't look like one.

"Mr Williams isn't well and so I will be taking this class for the next week" she continued.

I heard a groan go up from most of the other kids in the class. Except me of course. I smiled. Maybe my luck was changing.

"My name is Miss Simpson. So, I know you have your exams coming up in the next week, which means I need to hit the ground running if I am going to help you get prepared. I haven't had a chance to do a handover with Mr Williams. Can one of you maybe tell me what you are focussing on?"

Liam's hand shot straight up.

Once more I heard everyone groan.

Once more I didn't. What was wrong with them? I bet none of them was going to volunteer to update her. I certainly wasn't. Besides, Liam would probably do a better job that any of us could do.

Liam gave her a muttered overview of what we had covered. It was comprehensive, but definitely not succinct. He kept repeating himself and stumbling over the words. Miss Simpson was obviously getting impatient with him, but didn't want to just tell him to shut up.

Eventually he finished telling her everything we had done for the whole year, leaving out no detail.

Then, for the rest of the lesson, something very weird happened. I learnt stuff. It was like someone had taken a giant knotted ball of string and untangled it all in front of me. All that stuff I'd been really struggling to understand suddenly made total sense. It was amazing. She was amazing. Normally I hated being put on the spot by a teacher, but when she asked me a question, I enjoyed answering it. I could answer it. What made it even more amazing is that there were a couple of questions that Liam couldn't answer and I could. That was unheard of. Liam could always answer every question.

By the time the bell rang for the end of the day I had forgotten all the problems from the start of the day. It felt like, for the last couple of hours, I had been in a totally different reality. I hadn't noticed anything that Lisa was doing. I had only noticed Liam when Miss Simpson asked a question. And all the other kids in the class may as well not have been there. I even thanked the teacher as I left the class.

"You're welcome" she smiled "you clearly have an aptitude for maths"

I let out an involuntary snort.

"That's not what Mr Williams said" I told her.

"Really?" she said and then asked, "What is your name?"

"Emma" I answered.

Miss Simpson grabbed a pile of paper from the side of the desk and looked through it. I watched curiously. It appeared to be a pile of handwritten notes. I recognised the handwriting as being Mr Williams'.

"Emma, Emma…." She muttered to herself as she flicked through the paper.

"Ah yes, here we are…" and she took a moment to read the notes. I tried to read too but she was holding it at an angle that would have meant I had to lean right over her to see it. Bit too obvious!

She frowned.

'Oh God' I thought 'what has he said about me? She is gonna lecture me now isn't she?'

I took a deep breath and prepared myself for the standard "You have potential but you don't work hard enough" lecture.

"No" she looked up at me "he doesn't have much to say about you but it certainly doesn't say there are any problems". She turned the paper and showed it to me. "See?"

I read the paper.

"Emma. Perfectly capable. Just doesn't believe in herself so needs a little extra encouragement"

Extra encouragement? Is that what he called it? He was constantly on at me to work harder. He made me feel like I was stupid all the time.

"You seem surprised" said Mrs Simpson.

"Yeah, I am" I said. "I thought he really had it in for me".

Miss Simpson raised one eyebrow. I wasn't sure what that meant but realised I needed to get off to the bus, so told her thanks and headed out of the door towards the bus.

Lisa hadn't bothered waiting for me. I caught up with her as she nudged and pushed her way through the queue of people trying to get on the bus. It was always a bit of a scrap for the best seats at the end of the day. In the morning you didn't have a choice, it just depended on the order of the bus stops but at the end of the day it was a free-for-all. I'd experienced first-hand the effect of Lisa's elbows. She was very effective at cutting her way through the queue.

I followed in her wake, and suddenly remembered about losing my phone that morning. I wondered if my luck would continue to be in and if this was the same bus. I checked below the seat that Liam had been in, and sure enough, lying on the floor was my phone. With a huge sense of relief, I grabbed it and shoved it in my bag, quickly glancing around to make sure nobody (and especially not Lisa) noticed. Lisa still had her back to me as she headed to the back of the bus.

I needn't have worried. Lisa was, as usual, in her own little world. In fact, she was talking to me even though I wasn't behind her! I sat down next to her as she continued to waffle on. To be honest, I wasn't listening. I was so relieved to find my phone. I was also processing what Miss Simpson had shown me.

"Oi, I'm talking to you" said Lisa as she elbowed me in the side. I wish she'd stop doing that!

"Ow! What?" I snapped.

"Oooo moody!" Lisa teased. I hated it when she did that. She loved to make out that it was me being moody when she was being a cow.

"No. Not moody. Just fed up of you jabbing me in the ribs. Cut it out" It was unusual for me to say anything to her. Usually I just took whatever she said and apologised. But between them, Ninja and Caveman were making me look at everything in a different way. They had certainly shown me that there was more than one way of seeing things. For a moment, I wondered where they had been all day, but then I had another 'doh!' moment when I remembered that I hadn't had my phone all day.

"I was saying what a nightmare that Miss Simpson is" she continued, oblivious to my wandering thoughts. "She goes on and on and makes no sense at all. I'm well confused about maths now. If I fail my exam, it's her fault"

"I hate her" muttered Liam, who was sat in his usual place in front of us, on his own.

Lisa and I both shut up and stared. Liam never joined in our conversations. In fact, in all the time I'd known him, I could not remember ever hearing him offer his opinion on anything.

"You earwigging on our conversation?" Lisa asked, prodding his shoulder with her finger.

"Leave off him" I told her "he's allowed to talk"

Lisa looked at me like I'd just told her I was in love with Liam and we were going to get married and have babies.

"Gang up on me why don't you!" she said, "You and him best buddies all of a sudden now?"

"Get over it, Lisa" I said in an unusual moment of rebellion. "Besides, didn't you realise he was agreeing with you?"

Lisa looked at Liam and then at me. For once, she seemed at a loss for words.

After the day I'd had, I really couldn't be bothered with her drama so I decided to talk to Liam.

"Why do you hate her? I think she's awesome"

"She makes everything so confusing" he said "and she clearly has it in for me. She didn't even thank me for letting her know what we'd covered and then she kept picking on me with all the tricky questions. She gave you all the easy ones."

"She's just a cow. She clearly likes making students look stupid". Lisa had found her voice again. I wondered if she realised she was agreeing with Liam. The thought made me smile.

"You find that funny?" sneered Lisa "It's alright for you. Clearly she thinks the sun shines out of your butt!"

Liam sniggered. What was this? Liam and Lisa ganging up on me! Had I entered some weird sort of alternate reality? I was aware that my phone was buzzing away in my bag. I ignored it. If I pulled it out now it would just lead to a load of questions about who the messages were from, and I didn't want to share that with Lisa or with Liam.

Lisa and Liam continued to moan about Miss Simpson. You would think that Mr Williams was the most amazingly brilliant teacher and Miss Simpson was the spawn of Satan, based on their conversation. I decided to leave them to it. I, for one, was glad to see the back of Mr Williams, even if it was only for a few weeks. That was all the time I needed to get up to speed on my maths and do ok in my exam.

In no time at all I saw the familiar houses of my street and the bus came to its normal jerking halt at my bus stop. Lisa hadn't noticed. She was still fully engaged in slagging off teachers with Liam. I gave her a nudge with my elbow.

"Ow! What's up?" she snapped.

I tilted my head over to the door and pointed out that it was our stop. I checked my phone was still in my bag and stepped off the bus, being careful not to go flying down the steep step. Lisa followed behind, stumbling a little as she stepped down. I heard the muffled laughter of the other kids on the bus as the doors sighed shut.

"I'll see you later yeah?" said Lisa, as she tried to ignore the laughter.

Quite frankly, I wasn't in the mood for Lisa, or anyone.

"Sorry, no can do" I replied. I couldn't be bothered making an excuse so I just left it hanging there.

"Oh…right…fine then!" she said and stomped off to her house in a huff.

I could feel my phone buzzing in my bag again. I didn't bother looking at it. I didn't care about anything right now. I just wanted to get in, listen to some music and catch up with some YouTube videos and forget about everybody and everything for the rest of the day.

Because my mum wasn't at college, she'd made my favourite dinner. It smelled delicious and my stomach rumbled again. When she asked if I'd had a good day at school I shrugged and told her it was fine, and then escaped up to my room before my mother started asking me about Liam.

"Revision!" I shouted, as I headed up the stairs.

When I got up to my room I took a deep breath, and then pulled my phone out of my bag. I actually gave it a bit of a hug (sad I know) before I unlocked it and checked the messages.

What! 113 unread messages in WhatsApp. What on earth was going on?

Top of the list were Ninja and Caveman. I couldn't be bothered reading through the messages so I just started a group chat with them both.

Me: What the hell guys? What's with all the messages?

Caveman: OMG you were ignoring me. Why were you ignoring me? Anything could have happened. You could have died! I have been so worried about you. So much has happened; the teacher, the boy, the girl, all the other kids. ANYTHING COULD HAVE HAPPENED!

Ninja: You really shouldn't ignore me. I was just trying to help.

Me: I thought you knew everything that goes on in my head. I lost my phone. Turns out I dropped it on the bus. How come you didn't realise?

Caveman: Oh.

Ninja: Oh.

Ninja: Well we couldn't tell. I know how you are feeling but I can't see what you see. All I know is that when I talk, you get a message on your phone. So, I was talking. But you weren't responding on your phone. So much was happening. I thought you were just ignoring me. Or worse. I was kinda getting like Caveman and thinking something bad had happened. Although, I knew nothing had really happened cos I could still tell what was going on in your head.

Me: Everything is fine. You can chill now. I've got revision to do so can you shut up for a while do you think?

Caveman: Revision? You need to do that. If you don't do well at the exams there is no way you are gonna survive out there on your own.

Ninja: Oh shut up Caveman! She'll be fine. She'll do the best she can.

Me: Just so I'm clear, how is this shutting up?

I flicked my phone back onto silent and stuck it face down on my desk.

I looked at the pile of books. Maths was on the top. I really needed to study. I really, really should.

I rested my head on the desk and closed my eyes. I couldn't focus. I was tired. Maybe I should grab a granny nap before I started revising? Problem was, I always felt a bit rubbish afterwards if I slept in the afternoon.

"Come on Ems, focus" I said to myself.

It didn't work.

I picked up my phone again and started scrolling through Facebook. What on earth was that dog doing to that cat? So funny. Like. What else is going on? I can see Lisa is online. She's liking and sharing loads of posts. Commenting on a few too. Usually the ones where someone we know is looking stupid. Oh look, another selfie from Lisa with her boyfriend. He doesn't look too happy to be there. Like. I guess I wasn't the only one not getting much studying done.

Enough! I put my phone down on the desk again. This time I left it face up though. You know, just in case something really important came up. I looked at the pile of books again. Maybe I should start with something I liked, like Biology, or Art. But the Art exam was in the art room and all I had to do was draw. I could practice drawing though. That didn't require much brain power.

I started drawing. I really liked the cartoon style of drawing but I was rubbish at it. The teacher had said to try copying a few different styles so I Googled a few images and started copying them.

Soon it was late, and I was struggling to keep my eyes open. I didn't get any studying done. Ah well, I'll just have to do twice as much tomorrow evening.

WEDNESDAY: I'M SO FAT, I'LL NEVER GET A BOYFRIEND

I woke up feeling guilty. I really should have studied last night. The first exam is on Friday and I haven't prepared for it at all. My mother had one of her college days so I got up 10 minutes before the bus and got hair and makeup sorted without worrying about her telling me off for putting too much "slap" on. It also meant I didn't have to lie to her about not having breakfast. I'd come close to blowing it yesterday. I didn't think I'd have enough resolve for an argument with my mum.

I don't know why she was always on at me about eating enough. It was such double standards. For as long as I can remember she has been on a diet. She seems to have tried some really weird ones too. There was this one where all she did was drink soup. The soup smelt smelled vile. She kept going on at me to try it but there was no way! Especially as I could tell from the look on her face when she had it that it tasted as vile as it smelt smelled. Needless to say, she didn't stick to that for very long. I was glad too. The kitchen had become a no-go zone for me.

I didn't get why she was always on a diet. She looked fine to me. I think it was after my dad left that she started. I didn't really know my dad very well. He left when I was 3 and never really kept in touch. My mum said he would promise to come and take me out for the day, and I would get all excited and watch out of the window for hours. Sometimes he would call a few hours after he was due to pick me up and make some sort of excuse. Sometimes he didn't even bother with that.

It used to upset me a lot. I thought I was doing something wrong. Now I'm older I don't care about him at all. Well, I don't care as much as I did. I am happy with it being just me and mum. Every now and then, out of the blue, I get a birthday card from him. It's usually at least a week too late. He doesn't even put any money or anything in it. Mind you, that's probably a good thing. Once, when I was 13, he sent me a £10 ToysRus voucher in a Christmas card. Apart from the fact that there is nothing for a 13-year-old in a kids toy shop, even if there was, £10 wouldn't buy me a thing!

I do get sad thought when I see Lisa with her mum and dad. It feels like I'm missing out. I guess my dad just doesn't care enough about me to make an effort. If I ever have kids I will make sure I am with a guy that will stick around. Not that I'm planning on having kids. Ever!

I've always tried to make things easier for mum. It's kind of hard to tell how she feels about stuff because she doesn't really share very much. Her diets are the only way I have any clue that she's not very happy. She bangs on at me all the time saying "It doesn't matter what you look like Ems. Sometimes people are pretty on the outside and ugly on the inside and vice versa. If someone loves you, they love you for who you are, not how you look". Kind of hard to take her seriously though when all she ever seems to do is complain about how she looks.

My favourite time with my mum is when she's upset over something. That makes me sound mean doesn't it? But you see, when she's upset she likes to break out a tub of Ben & Jerry's Ice cream (Chocolate fudge brownie is my favourite) and we snuggle up under a duvet on the sofa and watch films on Netflix. For those few hours, nothing else matters. We could eat until we felt sick, watch films with adult content that she'd usually freak out about, and talk. We could talk about anything and I didn't feel like I was going to get in trouble.

I stood in front of the mirror and looked at myself in my school uniform. I had my skirt pulled up so it was as short as I could get away with. I put my hands on my hips and pushed down, out of some stupid belief that I could squash them down a bit. I then turned sideways on and breathed in as much as I could and put my shoulders back. It was no good, I couldn't make my bulging belly disappear. I read somewhere that you were fat if you didn't have a gap at the top of your thighs. I stood with my legs apart to try and create a gap. It was no use. I'd look like a right muppet if I walked like that. I needed to stick to my diet more. From today I would be super good and not eat any crap.

"Fat cow!" I muttered to the Emma in the mirror as I turned away from it and headed downstairs.

Today was a study day, so technically I didn't need to be in as early. The problem was, if I didn't catch the school bus, there was no real way for me to get into school so I had no choice but to get in at the same time as everybody else.

As I headed out of the door, I remembered that my phone was still on the desk upstairs so I legged it back to grab it. There was one message waiting for me.

Caveman: Excuse me. I'm a bit confused.

I ignored the message because I didn't want to miss the bus, and shoved my phone into my bag (carefully!) for later.

When the bus arrived, there was no sign of Liam in his usual seat. Lisa didn't dash through the doors at the last minute either, so I was all on my own. I looked around to see if people were still laughing at me, but nobody seemed to be paying me any attention, so I sat in my usual seat and took out my phone.

Me: What's up with you now?

Caveman: I'm trying to do my best to look after you but I can't work out if we are in a period of feast or a period of famine right now. I think it's famine because you're not eating much, but in the past you've done this and then eaten loads. I just need to sort your metabolism out.

I had no idea what he was talking about. Feast or Famine? I decided to see if Ninja could shed any light on what was going on. I would have just ignored him, but as I didn't have anyone else to talk to on the bus, I figured I may as well humour him.

Me: Ninja, what is he on about?

Ninja: He's a caveman. All he thinks about is survival. He can't help it. It's his programming.

Clear as mud. Really, these two were more hassle than they were worth.

Ninja: He's talking about your eating. He's in charge of your body and how it metabolises food. He uses signals from you and what you are doing to adjust your metabolism.

We covered this stuff in Biology. Not all the caveman stuff, but metabolism. I remember learning all about it and being frustrated because clearly my metabolism meant that every single thing I ate turned into fat. Whereas Lisa seemed to eat way more than me and was skinny as anything. It really wasn't fair. Now I knew who to blame: Caveman!

Right, if he cared about me as much as he said, it was about time he started helping me out.

Me: Which one would make me skinnier?

Caveman: Famine. But that's really bad. You can't survive if you are starving. Are you saying we are going to have a famine soon? I best stock you up if that is the case.

Oh god. I did not like the way the conversation was going.

Me: No! Stop. Don't do anything! I don't want to be any fatter. I'm already huge. Ninja – tell him!

Ninja: Maybe if you were just ok with you how you looked then Caveman could just back off and leave you to it? Nobody cares what you look like.

Geez, neither of them were making me feel any better about myself. Ninja was always banging on about how nobody cared about me. That was not very nice to hear. I know my dad didn't care. Clearly Lisa didn't care. But I'd always thought my mother cared about me. Maybe she didn't? If I wasn't so fat I was sure I'd fit in a lot better and people wouldn't treat me so horribly. Lisa was always pointing out the way other people looked and making fun of them. I didn't want her to do that about me when I wasn't around (or when I was!)

Me: Look, cut it out Caveman. If you want to help, stop me wanting to eat all the junk that makes me fat. Can't you stop me being hungry or something?

Caveman: Erm…well…you see it's tricky because you don't really ever get hungry. You just eat at all sorts of random times so I don't really know what's going on.

Well, that was rubbish. Clearly Caveman didn't know what he was talking about. I was always hungry. I am pretty sure if I wasn't hungry, it would be way easier to avoid eating.

Caveman: When did you last hear your stomach rumble?

Me: Ha! Yesterday! Told you that you didn't know me!

I was feeling quite smug. Caveman didn't know what he was on about. To make sure I won the point, I thought about other times I'd been hungry. There must be other times. I was always hungry. In fact, the reason I usually ended up eating junk was because I was hungry and couldn't be bothered to wait until a meal time. However, the more I thought about it, the more I realised that Caveman had a point. It had been quite a while since I'd been hungry. I'd skipped most meals for the last couple of weeks.

Caveman: See. Told you so. Now, when did you last eat until you felt sick?

That was easy. That happened all the time. My mum always told me that it was wasteful to put food on my plate and not finish it. It was especially hard if the food was really tasty. It seemed such a shame to waste tasty food. In my defence, I often ate when I was miserable. I needed chocolate! It's a well-known fact girls need chocolate. When I did eat, I would often overeat, like when my mum made my favourite meal. I told myself it was because my mum would be upset if I didn't, but it's just that it was so tasty, I hated to leave any. Once I started, I didn't seem to be able to stop. I'd eat a plate full of food and have pudding after, and probably have a snack later as well.

Caveman: See? It's impossible for me to know what to do. You always ignore me. I tell you to stop cos you're full but you carry on. I specifically don't tell you that you're hungry, but you still eat. How am I supposed to know what to do?

Me: Well you could give me a bit of help. If you are in control of this, give my metabolism a boost. Then it won't matter what I eat because my body will burn it all up instantly.

Caveman: But…but…but I can't!

Me: Why not?

Caveman: Because you'll die!

Oh man! He was off again.

Me: Yeah, I'll die of embarrassment because of my fat thighs and big fat butt and I will never get a boyfriend and my life will be over!

I was sure that's why I didn't have a boyfriend. Lisa had tried to set me up a couple of times. We'd double dated with one of her boyfriend's mates. It had always worked out as a disaster. One had been a right idiot. He kept doing stupid things and laughing his head off with Lisa's boyfriend about it. Lisa would laugh along too and then call me a grump for not joining in. It wasn't funny. The other hadn't said more than two words all evening – "hello" and "cya". I refuse to go on double dates any more. It's not worth the hassle.

The bus pulled up at school. I gave up on the pointless conversation with Caveman, stuck my phone on vibrate, and tucked it safely into my bag.

As there were no lessons, I headed straight for the library.

Liam was in the library, books out and head down. There was no signed of Lisa. He looked up and smiled when he saw me in the doorway. He then cleared his books from the space on the table next to him. 'Oh god' I thought 'he expects me to go and sit next to him, doesn't he?'

I realised there was no way of avoiding it. I didn't want to be mean to him but I also didn't really want to be seen next to him. I glanced around the library. Luckily it seemed that the other people I knew had decided to stay home and study. Reluctantly I took my bag off my shoulder and went and sat down next to Liam.

My phone buzzed.

We were allowed phones in the library but it was still frowned on. We were supposed to be there to work. I checked out the message, keeping it inside my bag to make it look like I was fetching my books out.

Ninja: Liam really likes you.

'Hah!' I thought. Problem was, I thought it a bit too loudly. Liam leant over to me:

"Who's that?" he whispered.

"Oh no one" I answered, frantically shoving my phone back in the back. The last thing I needed was for Liam to see that message.

Ninja was wrong. There was no way Liam liked me. He might see me as the only person that was actually willing to talk to him, but that's not the same as liking me.

Liam let out a sigh.

"What's up?" I asked.

"I really thought I understood this" he said pointing to the open page in a maths text book, "but after yesterday I don't think I do"

"Really? It's dead easy" I said and grabbed the book and started explaining it to him.

It was kinda tricky because he just kept sighing, and I swear it if he slumped down in his chair any more he'd be lying under the table. It struck me as quite amusing that I was there, in the library, trying to explain to Liam, the class swot, how to do maths. It was me that was more likely to mess up my exams.

We worked together all morning. I helped him with the bits he was stuck on and he helped me with the other bits (the bits Miss Simpson hadn't covered yet). At about 12 o'clock my stomach gave off the most massive rumble. I swear everyone in the library must have been able to hear it. Well, at least that proved Caveman wrong; my stomach did rumble sometimes.

Liam looked at me and smiled.

"We should take a break and get some lunch"

"No it's ok" I said "you go. I'm not really hungry, and anyway I have more revision to do. I'm not as smart as you"

Liam looked at me. He looked like he was about to say something, but then he lost his nerve and shrugged his shoulders and walked off.

I went back to reading the maths book. I must have read the same line at least 20 times and still couldn't tell you what it was about. My stomach was still rumbling and it was making it really hard to concentrate.

I sat back in my chair, keeping my arms round my stomach to try and muffle the sound. I nearly fell off my chair when I realised Liam was just standing there looking at me. I hadn't noticed him come back into the room.

"What the hell!" I whispered furiously.

"Look, you…erm…you ob…obviously don't l..l…like me" he stammered, not making eye contact with me. He tried staring at my middle but quickly looked away awkwardly and settled on staring at the book on the table.

"I..It's not really f..fair to string me along like this. If you didn't want to join me for lunch, there was no need to lie. You should've just said". The more he spoke, the more his voice steadied off.

I was shocked. Where did this come from? What on earth had I done? I started to get quite cross. I'd just spent the whole morning working with him and helping him out with stuff, and here he was throwing out a bunch of random accusations about me not liking him. The thing that annoyed me most was that he hadn't just spoken to me. He'd just made an assumption. I think I also felt a little guilty, because last week it would have actually been true; I didn't like him. But it was different now. He was a really sweet guy.

"Geez Liam. What's up with you?" I snapped defensively "I've just spent the morning working with you. You walk out the library and enter an alternative reality or something?"

Liam sat down next to me again. For a while neither of us said anything. I was working my way back through everything that happened over the last couple of days, trying to work out why Liam felt this way. Eventually Liam was the first to speak:

"I've enjoyed studying with you today" he muttered, quieter than was necessary to fit in with the rules of the library. "I've liked you for a long time, but you've never even spoken to me before. It's like I was invisible"

I felt guilty again for thinking of him as a creep.

"You're wrong" I replied "you weren't invisible. It's just we seemed so different. You have always been good at everything. The teachers think the sun shines out of your butt."

Liam smiled, and then instantly went back to looking very serious again.

"I just had no reason to speak to you before. But what you did for me on the bus the other day was really sweet. And then when you came round to my house yesterday, that was really thoughtful" ('and a bit creepy') I thought, then instantly felt guilty for it.

"Sweet?" asked Liam. But he wasn't looking for an answer. "Figures..." he trailed off back into his own thoughts.

I was getting seriously confused. I didn't know what he was after or what I was doing or saying wrong. I meant what I said. Liam had really surprised me over the past couple of days. He'd made some difficult stuff easier and I was grateful for that. I no longer thought of him as creepy. He seemed more like a good friend now. Weird how things can change so much in just a couple of days eh?

"Liam, I like you" I continued.

His face lit up and he looked right at me.

"I think we make good friends, don't we?" I asked.

He looked back at the book. I was sure if he closed his eyes he could recreate every contour of that book, he was staring at it so hard.

"Friends?" he asked, "I guess so." And he continued to stare at the book.

I sighed. I was exasperated. I really didn't understand boys!

"What made you think I didn't like you?" I asked to break yet another awkward silence.

He looked at me again:

"You said you weren't hungry when I asked you to join me for lunch, but you obviously are because your stomach rumbled. It was so loud I'm surprised the teacher didn't tell you to keep the noise down!"

I smiled. I'd had the same thought when it first rumbled!

Why did he have to make this about him? It was nothing to do with him. Now I was in an awkward position. I didn't want to make Liam think I didn't want to be friends with him. Then again, I wasn't sure I wanted to let him know the real reason I wasn't joining him for lunch.

Just then, my phone vibrated a couple of times. I could have sworn I put it on silent.

Ninja: Told you he liked you.

Me: Yeah, you were right. He's actually a pretty good mate. Not like I thought he was at all.

Ninja: <Face, Palm> No. He **likes** you.

Caveman: Yay, Emma has a boyfriend. Emma has a boyfriend. Now, tell him you really like him before he goes off with some other girl.

I felt my face going red. These guys were impossible. But when I thought about it, it kind of made sense. If it was just about not going to lunch, then Liam's response would be way over the top. But if he was interpreting it as me not liking him, then I guess I could understand his reaction.

I sighed and looked over at Liam. He was spinning a pen on the table and staring at the book.

"I'm sorry Liam. It's not about you. I just don't want to eat lunch and I

51

didn't want to tell you cos I was kind of embarrassed"

Liam looked confused.

"Why would you be embarrassed about eating lunch? Do you not like people watching you eat? I wouldn't watch."

Liam was clearly clutching at straws. He didn't know what it was like to have to worry about how you looked all the time.

My phone buzzed. Liam gave me an evil stare as if to say "don't you dare look at that". But I had to look.

Ninja: Liam worries about his looks just as much as you.

I snorted out a suppressed laugh.

Me: Seriously, what do boys know about having to look good? Liam is lovely but he's scruffy as hell. Although, he does smell quite nice.

I sniffed. Liam looked at me funny.

Ninja: Don't you think he smells nice because he cares what he smells like. To you.

I looked at Liam again. He had gel in his hair. I hadn't noticed that before. I'm sure I'd never seen him with gel in his hair before. Come to think of it, his clothes didn't seem quite as scruffy as I remembered them before. Maybe I just remembered it wrong?

Liam shifted in his seat uncomfortably.

"What? What's wrong?" he asked.

It struck me, in that moment, as I worried what Liam thought about my behaviour, that I spent a lot of time worrying what other people thought of me. And the crazy thing, is that I was almost always wrong. If that was true of me, it was just as true for Liam. He was a mile off with the reason why I didn't go for lunch with him. He'd got himself all worked up based on what he thought was right in his head. It was nothing to do with the reality.

Ninja: There you go, now you're cottoning on.

If a random invisible person in WhatsApp could sound proud, I guessed that Ninja was sounding proud in that moment. I smiled.

My stomach rumbled again. This was probably the loudest it had rumbled so far. Instead of being embarrassed this time, I laughed. Liam looked at me, and smiled a bit, as if to test that he wasn't going to get into trouble. Then, when it rumbled again we both burst out laughing.

"Shhhhh!" hushed the teacher supervising the library.

Liam tipped his head to suggest we leave the library. I agreed. I shoved my stuff in my bag, including my phone and followed him out. We stood in the corridor outside and just lost it. Everyone must have thought I was a total loon, but in that moment, I didn't care.

"So why aren't you eating lunch?" Liam asked, after he finished laughing "and don't tell me that it's because you're not hungry because I know for sure that's a lie!"

I smiled, took a deep breath and then told him. Give him credit, he looked properly shocked. I liked him a little bit more for that. I was quite amused by how hard he was trying to not look at my legs when I was telling him about my fat thighs. It probably didn't help that I was grabbing lumps of flesh there and wobbling them as an illustration of the point I was trying to make.

The thing was, I was actually about to cave in and get something to eat. I told myself I couldn't concentrate properly on all the study I had to do if my blood sugar was too low (something else I'd learnt in Biology). I was giving myself lots of reasons that I should eat. Caveman had given me another reason. I didn't want him taking me into that mode where he slowed my metabolism down. What did he call it? Starvation? Fasting? Something like that anyway. However, I'd backed myself into a corner telling Liam about it. If I joined him for lunch now, he'd think I was just telling him all that stuff to make him feel better.

I decided to change topic and see if I could distract myself from my rumbling stomach.

"Such a pain having to catch the bus. I'm not sure how much more my brain can absorb. I wish we could just go home."

"We could catch a regular bus" suggested Liam.

I shook my head.

"I'm broke" I said. I was just about to tell him I spent the last of my money on a bunch of junk food the other day, when I realised that would also make him feel bad about lunch today. So, I left it at that.

"No problem" he replied, pulling some crumpled money out of his pocket. A bunch of coins fell to the floor as he unfolded the notes to see how much he had. "This should be enough for both of us".

I bent down to help him pick up the coins. He was being nice to me again.

"I don't even know what bus to take." I was deflecting again. I really wanted to take him up on his offer, but I felt bad because I'd spent all my money on rubbish food.

"Don't worry, I do" he said as he picked up the last of the coins. "I take it all the time in the morning because my dad..." he went quiet "...anyway I've taken the one into school but never the one home but it shouldn't be much different"

We felt a bit naughty leaving school in the middle of the day. It was ok though. It was a study day and technically we didn't even have to go in in the first place. We chatted as we walked down the hill from school into town. The bus stop was opposite a chip shop. That was rubbish planning that was!

"I'm starving. I'm gonna grab some chips. Do you want some?" he asked.

I shook my head.

"It's ok" he said "my shout".

"Nah, best not I said" while my head screamed at me to say yes.

When he disappeared off, my phone started buzzing.

Caveman: Eat some food! You are going to starve to death!

Ninja: I hate to agree with him but Caveman is right. I think you'll find Liam doesn't really care what you look like. If he did, he wouldn't have looked so shocked when you said you were fat. Just let him buy you some chips.

This was proving impossible. Everyone except me thought I should have some chips.

Liam wandered out of the chip shop with his bag of chips open, picking away at them. I almost had to wipe drool from the side of my mouth, it was watering so much. Not an attractive look at all. Although I wasn't sure why I cared. Before I could follow that train of thought, Liam was stood next to me and had stuck the bag of chips under my nose. I didn't even realise that I'd reached out and grabbed one, until I swallowed it. Oh god, what I had done? That chip would get metabolised straight into fat. I sat on my hands to stop myself accidentally grabbing any more. Out of what had been a pretty rotten few days, this moment was pretty good. Liam seemed happy to sit next to me eating chips. I occasionally reached and grabbed one, then surreptitiously chucked it behind me. The pigeons would enjoy them later. He didn't seem to notice, which was good. He was actually one of those skinny people that annoyed me so much. He could eat junk like chips not have to worry about his thigh gap like I did.

In that moment though, I didn't care. All that mattered was that I was on my way home, and I was with someone who was actually being nice to me.

I don't know how much time passed before the bus arrived. We seemed to have hardly spent any time waiting and yet the chips were finished and the empty paper was in the bin across the road. I noticed Liam wipe his greasy hands down his trousers. I guess I should have been grossed out by that, but I'd just done the same. The difference was, all my chips were behind the bus stop. I glanced at them guiltily and then looked away quickly before Liam noticed.

When the bus arrived, we got on and went straight up to the top deck. It felt weird to sit in a different part of the bus. We had our routines for the school bus and it was generally accepted that you always sat in the same place with the same people. Once more, it felt like I was doing something wrong, even though I wasn't. We were like giggly little kids sat at the front on the top deck, drawing pictures in the condensation on the window.

It was a lot quicker to get home on this bus. It took quite a different, more direct, route and didn't stop as many times as the school bus.

Soon we were getting off at the stop near my house. It seemed normal that Liam got off the bus with me. When we reached my front door, I asked if he wanted to come in and do a bit of study. I felt I had enough brain power now after eating a couple of the chips!

"Sure" he shrugged, and followed me in. My mum was sat on the sofa with her laptop on her knee. She must have been doing some college work, or chatting to friends on Facebook. I hoped she wasn't tagging me in embarrassing photos again. She had a nasty habit of doing that. The place was silent. I never understood how she could do anything without music. I always listened to music while I did homework.

"Hey Ems, what are you doing home at…" she stopped when she saw Liam and her face lit up. Her voice also changed to her special visitor voice (it had started out as her 'telling you off' voice) "Oh hello Liam. I didn't notice you there. You are awful quiet"

"Mum!" I huffed. "You're embarrassing me"

Liam just smiled.

"It's a study day because we have our first exam on Friday so we're going upstairs ok?"

"Sure hun" my mum winked. Honestly. This is why I didn't usually invite boys home. Well, that and the fact that I'd never known a boy that actually wanted to come into my house before. Anyway, that was by-the-by, we headed upstairs.

Just as we reached my room my mother shouted up, inviting Liam for dinner.

"Erm…no. Sorry. I can't. My dad needs me back home."

We got into my room.

"I don't mind you staying" I said, "My mum's a pretty good cook"

"I c...can't" Liam seemed to have closed down again. He'd been chatting away on the bus. I noticed his stammer only appeared when he was nervous. I wasn't quite sure why talking about going home made him that way, but I certainly wasn't going to push him on it.

"No problems. What shall we study next then?"

We spent the next couple of hours studying various topics. It worked well. We supported each other's weaknesses with our strengths.

When it got near to 4pm, Liam looked out of my bedroom window and saw the school bus pull up at the stop. He frantically gathered his stuff together and shoved it unceremoniously in his bag.

"Gotta go" he said. "See you tomorrow?"

"Sure" I replied. I was a bit confused with what the rush was, but followed him down the stairs and waved goodbye as he headed off in the direction of his house. Weird guy.

When I came back into the living room, my mother was grinning from ear to ear.

"Sooo...Liam" she said teasingly.

I rolled my eyes, but instead of storming off I smiled.

"He's a pretty nice guy" I said. "We got a lot done today"

"I'm sure!" said my mother in a knowing way.

I rolled my eyes again.

When Lisa knocked on my door later that evening, books in hand, asking to study, I told her no. I told her I'd got loads done today and was going to take the evening off to watch Netflix with my mum.

Lisa stood on the doorstep for a second. It was almost like she didn't believe me and thought I was going to say "ha! Joke!" and invite her in. But I didn't.

"Fine!" she said and turned around and stormed off.

This would normally have bothered me and I would have chased after her and told her to come over, even though I didn't need to study. However now I just recognised that it was her problem and not mine.

I had a nice relaxing evening in with my mother, watching Netflix and pretending to eat Ben & Jerry's ice cream, while actually letting her eat most of it.

Weirdly, I'm looking forward to going to school tomorrow.

THURSDAY: I'M GOING TO LIVE WITH MY MUM FOREVER

I have no idea why I was so optimistic yesterday. How could I forget about my exams? Tomorrow my whole future will be decided. My whole life is going to be messed up because of 2 hours. What is the point of exams anyway? Why do we have to prove we can remember stuff? My mum says they weren't even allowed to use calculators in their exams. What's the point of that? Apparently, the teacher always said, "You won't have a calculator with you wherever you go so you need to learn to do sums in your head". Well duh! I have a calculator on my iPhone so I always have one.

If I don't get a good enough grade in maths then most of the Uni courses I might want to take won't accept me. They need maths and English. I'm ok at English so not too worried about that. Maths is a different kettle of fish. The time we spent in class with Miss Simpson was not enough to cancel out a whole year of confusion from Mr Williams.

I am doomed.

I talked to my mum about it this morning, because I was really freaking out.

She told me (again) how she messed up the first time. She was far more interested in boys and hanging out with her friends. While her friends went to college and Uni, she got a job. Then she got pregnant and had me and her life was all about looking after me. She looked into the distance wistfully at this that point.

"I really wish I could go back and do it over again. If I could I would work hard the first-time round. It's so much harder now"

Helpful. Not. My mother reminding me again that she regretted having me was not helpful. Plus, I was feeling under even more pressure now about the exams.

"But don't worry, these mock exams are just practice. They're a good chance to practice and learn how to study. It doesn't matter if you mess up as long as you learn something from it" she said.

Yeah, they may only have been the mock exams but you would think they were just as, if not more, important than the final exams if you listened to the teachers. All they had gone on about for the last few months was how important it was to do well in our exams. In every lesson, the teacher would be like "this may well be in the exam. Nudge, Nudge, Wink, Wink." Mum said it was crazy because we were at school to learn stuff, that was the whole point. Going on at us to make sure we knew everything and didn't get anything wrong was a bit daft.

The one thing my mother had always told me was to ignore it when I got in trouble for not knowing the answer to something, because that was bad teaching and nothing to do with me. I learned a lot from a thing that happened when I was in primary school and way behind on my times tables. I was about 8 and the other kids in my year were on their 6 times table. I kind of got it, but I kept being put back to my 4 times table because I couldn't instantly answer the teacher's questions. I felt really stupid. I was clearly no good at maths. Everyone else seemed to find it so much easier to learn their times tables than me. I used to tell my mother I was ill on the days where I knew we had maths. She didn't buy it. She just told me that my tummy was telling me what my head was feeling, and that I would be ok when I got to school. I wasn't ok when I got to school. But I gave up trying to get off school because it never worked. Just like on Tuesday actually!

One day we got a student teacher. She taught me a different way of learning my times tables that was more about rhythm and singing. I loved that. I always loved to sing and dance when I was little. In fairness, I still do, but now I do it on my own in my room rather than in the living room in front of everybody. That would be totally humiliating!

After that, stuff got a lot easier because, with my mums help, I just found a way that worked for me and blamed the teacher for bad teaching if I didn't get it.

That did get me in a fair bit of trouble at primary school though. My mum would get called in because I was disrupting the class. Firstly, I wasn't like the other kids; I didn't care what the teacher thought of me. I didn't worry about being told off. My mother had done too good a job on me! And then there was the fact that I loved making everyone laugh. I was definitely the class clown when I was in Primary school. When did that change? High school. Everything changed in High school. We still had a class clown. It just wasn't me. It was Grayson. Most of the time we all just rolled our eyes at him, but in reality, we were often quite glad of the interruption. Like me when I was at Primary School, Grayson didn't seem too worried about getting in trouble for his antics.

Anyway, when I was still the class clown and the teacher got frustrated at me for being disruptive, I would take it a bit too literally that it was her problem not mine. If she couldn't control the class, that was her problem. I was only 8, in my defence! Whenever her back was turned I would make everyone laugh, and then they would all get in trouble for being disruptive. My mother got so fed up with my bad reports that she eventually told me that I could do whatever I wanted as long as I didn't get caught. It's an interesting life lesson. I'm not sure it will work so well when I'm an adult, but it was great when I was younger. I was smart, so was able to avoid getting caught most of the time.

It's weird, now I look back on that. I wonder when I stopped being that kid? What would happen if I treated Mr Williams the same way as I treated my primary school teacher? There was certainly a good argument for it. Miss Simpson had shown that it was his rubbish teaching and not my stupidity that had led to me struggling with maths. Up until I had him I had no problems at all with it. God, why on earth did I not realise that until the day before my exam? Why did my mum not remind me of that too? Mind you, now I think about it, I probably haven't told her. We really didn't talk any more. My school parent's evenings were always fine. The teachers had so many kids to talk about that they only remembered the ones that stood out as being particularly good or particularly bad. I was neither. My mum would spend 2-3 minutes with each of my teachers and they usually had very little to say. I'm not sure they even remembered who I was to be honest. All, that is, apart from my Art teacher, Mrs Wilson. She would spend 15-20 minutes raving on at my mum about how brilliant I was and how much potential I had. Mrs Wilson told my mother that if she had half my talent when she was my age, she would definitely not be teaching. She would be making a living from selling her art. It was seriously embarrassing. Although a part of me loved it too. I would watch my mother almost glow with pride.

I wasn't worried about my Art exam. I'd already done enough to get a C from my coursework alone. Besides, I had no interest in doing art as a career, no matter what Mrs Wilson said. You couldn't make money from being an artist. All I had to do was spend half a day in the art classroom drawing to complete the exam and get my predicted A+. If anything, I was looking forward to that exam! Unfortunately, it was the last exam of all of them. It was all the others that scared the hell out of me.

My whole life is going to be ruined because I am rubbish at exams. My biggest worry is that I will miss a whole page of questions or mis-read a question. I have no attention to detail. I never do very well at homework assignments. I don't fail them or anything, but I never get the best mark either. I guess that's why Mr Williams always seems so disappointed in me. Maybe he thinks I am just too lazy to try. Maybe he's right. Maybe if I tried harder I would do better. I am destined to be a failure for the rest of my life. I will do what my mum did and leave school, get a job and have babies. I will live with my mother and everybody will think I'm useless. And they'll be right!

My mother showed me this video on YouTube the other day, about all these people who were mega famous and rich, who were classed as failures when they were younger. Did you know that the guy who invented the glue on post-it notes was trying to invent a proper glue? I think it was even supposed to stick aircraft parts together. He messed up, but we got post-it notes. I love post-it notes. I love the little tiny ones you can stick in books. I have spent hours getting ready to study by marking all the important stuff in my books and my notes using little post-it notes. I probably should spend more time studying. I guess that's just another example of how lazy I am. It just seems easier to mess around with post-it notes and marker pens, than to study.

Maybe that's just me. Lisa has always made fun of me for my study charts and post-its. She doesn't seem to have any structure to her study. She does a lot more than me though. She has to. Her dad is on her case all the time. Her dad is some sort of lawyer. He isn't home much and always seems to be in court. He's even on TV a fair bit apparently. He wants Lisa to do the same thing. He thinks it's important that she gets good grades and goes on to study law at Uni. It doesn't seem to matter what Lisa wants. When she goes out with her boyfriend, she often tells her parents she's coming over to mine to study. I hate that she puts me in a position where I have to lie for her, but then again, I don't think it's fair for her dad to pressure her like that. Whatever I say about my mum, she at least lets me make my own choices.

ping

"Who's that? Liam?" my mum asked.

"Erm…yeah" I lied. I figured that would be easier than trying to explain the two strange men I talked to every day!

"Awww bless him" she cooed "answer him then. I'll go make us a coffee" and then she headed off to the kitchen. My mum drank a lot of coffee. I didn't have the heart to tell her I didn't really like coffee. I would just take the cup off her and then 'forget about it' until it was too cold to drink. Sometimes she'd call my bluff and offer to nuke it in the microwave but I would tell her that made it taste funny. She would nod knowingly.

Ninja: Do you really think you could try harder?

Me: I guess so. Maybe I wouldn't make so many mistakes? I think I'm just too lazy to be bothered.

My mum says I have the attention span of a gnat. I get bored so easily, and I get distracted easily too. Unless I'm drawing. I get totally lost in drawing and time seems to pass without me noticing.

I'm not sure what I want to do at Uni, but I know that I do want to go. It's the best chance I have of leaving home. My mum loves it now. I think she might still be at Uni when I go. That's just weird. Although my plan is to go to one that is far away, if I can afford it.

I just needed to stop all the procrastination and get down to some study. I had no plans to go into school today. It was my last chance to study before the maths exam.

Just then, my mother wandered back into the room.

"Is Liam coming over again to do some studying?" smiled my mother.

She put particular emphasis on the word 'studying'. Geez she was so embarrassing. She had a point though. It would be good to study with Liam. If nothing else, he would keep me on track. Problem was, I had no way of getting in touch with him. Whatever my mother thought, I didn't have him on WhatsApp, and he'd already told me that he didn't use Social Media. I didn't know where he lived because he always got off the bus after me.

"Erm…no…I don't think so. We did quite a lot yesterday. And he has subjects I don't have that he wanted to study for"

Just then, someone knocked at the door. Thinking it was Lisa, I went and hid in the kitchen and whispered to my mother to tell her I wasn't in. She gave me a confused look, and went and answered the door.

"Oh, hi Liam. I thought you weren't coming over today. I don't think Ems is in right now" my mother said, dutifully allowing me to hide in the kitchen. Except that I was no longer hiding in the kitchen. As soon as I heard Liam's name I had dashed over to the front door.

"Liam! Hi! Come in" I said as I grabbed the sleeve of his coat and dragged a very confused looking Liam into the house. I dashed upstairs, indicating that he should follow me, before my mother said anything more and exposed my lie.

We got to my room and I shut my door.

"Erm…I was just coming round to see if you wanted to study again" said a slightly shell-shocked Liam, who was now standing awkwardly by my bedroom door, looking around the room.

"Yeah I do" I replied "Although I'm not sure there is any point. I am so going to mess up. It doesn't seem to matter how hard I study, I never do very well"

Whilst these were the first proper exams I had taken, I had done loads of tests before. I used to do dance competitions when I was younger. I only stopped dancing when I got to high school. I didn't like wearing those tight costumes. I felt everyone was looking at me. I was always fatter than the other girls too. At first I didn't care, but when my shape changed I became very self-conscious. My mother had a bit of a rant at me about all the money she'd spent on me over the years, but it made no difference. No way I was humiliating myself that way. Can you imagine what Lisa would say behind my back?

The thing was, I was sick before every competition. I was always sick before any sort of test, in fact. I just knew I was gonna mess up and let everyone down. I used to persuade myself that it would be better if I never tried, than to mess up and have everyone realise how rubbish I really was. Weirdly, I used to forget about the nerves once I started and often got second or third place. I rarely got first place. I wasn't aware that my mum was a pushy mother. She always used to say, "just do your best" when I was scared before going on stage, and told me I was great whenever I came off. But I knew it cost her a lot (mainly because she always told me!) and as I got older and didn't enjoy it as much, it didn't seem right that she would struggle to pay for my various trips to competitions.

I know my mum said that I should just try my best and that was ok, but I wasn't really trying my best was I? If I would just focus I am sure I could do better.

Liam came in and sat down next to me on the bed. We didn't have a big house so my room was quite small. There was just about enough room for my bed, a small bedside table, a desk and something for my clothes. I insisted on a wardrobe because I wanted the full-length mirror and my mum told me that I couldn't fit that next to a chest of drawers. I didn't hang any of my clothes up in it. I couldn't be bothered with that.

It did mean that when I had friends round we ended up sitting on the bed together. I never really noticed with Lisa, but I was suddenly very aware that I now had a boy sitting next to me on my bed. Oh god, if anyone in school ever found out, I'd be ribbed something rotten. I'd probably never, ever live that down.

"My parents couldn't care less what I do" said Liam "My older brother messed up everything at school and now goes from job to job. He seems to last a couple of weeks, spend all his money on going out with his mates, and then gets fired and spends a couple of weeks doing nothing at home. My dad says we're both useless good-for-nothings. I suppose I'll just end up like my brother one day."

I never knew that about Liam. How could his dad call him useless? Liam was good at everything. If I was as useless as Liam, I'd be happy!

"What does your dad actually do?" I asked, thinking that his father must have some really high powered job to look down on his brother like that.

"Oh, nothing really" he shrugged "he says he is a carer for my mother. But he doesn't seem to do anything for her."

"Oh. Sorry to hear about your mum. What's up with her?" I asked, rather hesitantly. This conversation was taking quite an unexpected, deep turn.

"Not sure" he stared at a spot on the carpet so determinedly that I looked to see what he was staring at. I couldn't see anything. "She's in and out of hospital. Not the local, regular hospital. A special one"

He looked straight at me with that hurt puppy look again. I couldn't face talking about this anymore. I think he meant the mental hospital. We called it the nut house. I didn't feel like asking him to clarify though so I changed the subject.

"Well, this maths stuff. I don't get any of it, apart from the stuff Miss Simpson covered. I am going to fail, and end up living at home with my mother forever." I flung my arms down to my side dramatically to emphasise the point, but accidentally ended up brushing his leg at the same time.

As if on cue, my mother yelled up the stairs offering us both a coffee.

I yelled 'no' so firmly and loudly that I felt Liam physically jump next to me. I put my arm on his arm and apologised.

And there it was, my first 'moment' with a boy. In Hotel Transylvania, they call it a 'Zing'. Oh my god, I've just admitted to watching Hotel Transylvania. I love that film. I have watched it a million times. I just love Mavis. I want to be like her. I could live with being a vampire (excuse the pun!) Vampires get to fly places, and move really fast so I wouldn't have to go on the stupid bus. Of course, I wouldn't be able to go to school or work in a regular day job either. Actually, right now, that was an appealing prospect. I'd thought about it quite a lot. I'd been into vampires for years. Not the stupid sparkly Twilight vampires. Proper ones that were evil and mean. I worked out that I could stay alive by only killing the mean people in the world. It would be like I was a super-hero, saving the world for from horrible people. And I would never have to take an exam ever again.

Liam had clearly felt the zing too. He looked at me, looked at my hand that was still on his arm (why?) and looked at me again. Then he smiled.

My mind was in overdrive. What should I do? Maybe I should message Lisa and ask her. She had loads of experience with boys. But no, this was Liam. She would just make fun of me and not be helpful at all. Besides, I needed to move my hand to type a message. Would Liam read more into it if I left my hand there or took it away? What did I want him to think? What should I do? Arghhhhh!

Suddenly, the exam seemed to be the least of my worries.

Liam was still looking at me. He wasn't smiling any more. What was he thinking? Was he thinking I was weird for putting my hand on his arm? Did he want me to take it away or leave it there?

Liam leaned over to me. His face was right next to mind. Oh god, he was going to kiss me. And I wanted him to kiss me. As he leaned in closer, our noses banged into each other. I muttered "sorry" awkwardly. He didn't stop. Thank goodness, he didn't stop! We both turned our heads and tried again. Unfortunately, we turned them the same way and banged noses again. I giggled.

Just then, the door to my bedroom door opened. It was my mother.

"I don't care if you are here with a boy" she said, pointing her finger crossly "that is no excuse to talk to me like that!"

Then she went quiet. She had noticed the position I was sat in, with Liam right next to me on the bed and my hand on his arm, our faces close to each other. Her mouth hung open for a moment, then she turned and walked out of the room. Just as she turned to leave, I could see the smile on her face.

I used the interruption as an excuse to move back a bit.

Liam cleared his throat, and picked up the maths book.

"So, erm, which bit do you want to work on first?" he asked.

We spent the next hour studying. Liam was a surprisingly good and patient teacher.

When I heard Liam's stomach rumbling, I realised that we had lost all track of time while we were studying, and it was now well past lunchtime.

"Sorry" Liam apologised "I guess I'm hungry. We can go get a bag of chips if you like? I'm sure we could both use a break and a bit of fresh air"

Oh God, chips twice in one week. I was going to be huge. I'd be the kid that had to go buy my clothes in the 'special' shops because nothing from the regular shops fit me. I really wanted to say no. Yet, I really needed a break and right in that moment, I couldn't think of anything better to do than to share a bag of chips with Liam. I hadn't understood a thing for the last 30 minutes anyway. My stomach had started rumbling before his. It's just he was so caught up with the maths problem that he hadn't noticed. Or maybe he had, and was just too polite to say anything.

Somehow, in the course of studying, we had ended up closer to each other on the bed. Our arms were now fully connected. Liam smelt nice. I loved the way he smelled. I panicked. Had I put deodorant on this morning? I might not have. I was so busy freaking out about the exam that I hadn't even put make up or anything on. Maybe Liam was thinking I was smelly? But wouldn't he have said something if that was the case.

ping

I hadn't checked my phone all morning, not since the messages when I was talking with my mum.

I daren't read the message while sat so close to Liam. Even if he wasn't trying, he'd be able to see the whole conversation easily.

I stood up and said I just needed to pop to the toilet. I grabbed my phone, and slightly awkwardly, moved away from him on the bed so he wouldn't fall over when I stood up. I knew I had a spare deodorant in the toilet so I could check my messages and freshen up at the same time.

ping

Two messages. Ok, what had I missed?

Caveman: This is good. I'm very happy that you have a boyfriend now. Now if you can just make sure you eat enough, we'll be all good.

What? Liam wasn't my boyfriend! Caveman had totally got it wrong. Besides, what if we were really good friends? It was none of his business.

Ninja: Remember, you can't read minds. If you want to know what Liam thinks, just ask him. Oh, and don't worry about your exam. You will do your best. To believe anything else would mean you believed in time travel. You don't do you?

Me: Of course I don't. I have literally no clue what you are talking about right now. If I don't study hard enough, of course I won't do my best. My best would be to study really hard, spend time on the questions, and get a really good score.

Ninja: Yes. But even if you don't do that, you can't change time. There are no do-overs. So it's still going to be your best.

Me: What are you on about? Honestly, you guys really need to get a life and stop going on at me.

Caveman: You are my life.

Ninja: You are my life.

Caveman, Ninja: Jinx!

Honestly! They are so childish. Why was I even bothering listening to them?

I switched my phone to silent and shoved it back in my pocket. Carefully. I knew from painful experience that you need to be careful when you are using your phone near the toilet. Amazingly, sticking it in a bag of rice on the radiator overnight sorted it out. But there is no way I was risking that again!

I didn't want to spend too long in the toilet. That would make Liam think there was something wrong with me.

Sod it. I was hungry and I needed a break. When I got back in the room, Liam had packed away all the books and was just sitting there waiting for me.

"Let's go" I said "I'm starving. Oh, but I still don't have any money. Maybe I can ask my mother for some?"

"Don't worry" said Liam "I'll cover you. Least I can do after you helping me to study"

Me helping him? That was not how I saw it. Maybe Ninja had a point. Maybe we did see things differently.

"Sure?" I asked. He nodded. We headed out. My mother was obviously sulking at me because she didn't say a thing when I yelled through that we were off out to grab some lunch. I'd have to sort that out later. Right now, I had other, more important, things on my mind.

We walked along the road in silence at first. Then I was aware that Liam kept glancing at me, as if he was about to say something. It was getting quite annoying so I asked him what was up.

"I like you Emma" he said hesitantly. He couldn't look me in the eyes while he talked. He kept staring at one spot on the pavement.

I swear my heart physically jumped when he said that. This was the first time in my entire life I remember a boy telling me he liked me. A boy liked me. A boy that had seen me fill my fat face with chips. A boy that I'd been horrible to and thought mean things about. A boy that had always been there, but that I'd never noticed. He liked me. And actually, I quite liked him too.

"You can call me Ems" I said, "it's only teachers that call me Emma".

He still didn't look at me.

"And I like you too" I smiled. He looked at me then, and had the biggest smile on his face. I didn't need to read minds to know that was as much a smile of relief as it was of happiness.

He reached out and took my hand. His hand was clammy, and a little unpleasant to hold. Yet, at the same time, it made my heart flutter again. I was walking down the street with a boy, holding hands. Yes, me!

We turned the corner to the row of shops where the "Cheerful Chipper" was. It was my local chipshop and they did pretty good chips. Unfortunately. At least if they had been rubbish I wouldn't have had them so often!

We both spotted Lisa and let go of each other's hand at the same time. I don't think either of was ready to deal with Lisa's mockery just yet. She hadn't noticed us. In fact, she didn't notice us until we were right next to her and I said hello.

When she turned to say hi back, I could see something was up. Her face was blotchy and her eyes were red. I looked at Liam and he understood.

"Catch you later Emm…Ems" he said, and headed into the chip shop. My stomach rumbled in protest at not following him in. But I couldn't turn my back on Lisa. She was my friend after all.

I waited for Liam to disappear and then I asked her what was up.

"Stu has dumped me" she said, clearly struggling to hold it together. A tear trickled down her cheek and she casually brushed it away.

I was really surprised. She'd been with Stuart for ages. She'd always talked to me about the big plans they both had for their life together when they left school. Of course, her dad didn't know anything about the relationship. He would have gone spare if he thought anything was taking her away from her studies. He would also have gone spare if he'd heard any of the plans she'd made with Stuart. None of them involved a law degree. Stuart was good looking, sure enough. He was on the school football team so was a perfect match for Lisa. She was a popular girl, and he was a popular boy.

"What are you doing here?" I asked her, scrabbling around in my pocket for a tissue.

"I can't go home" she sobbed "I can't stop crying and if my dad sees me like this he'll ask me what's up. He'll go totally mental if he finds out about Stu".

I looked wistfully over at the chip shop, then suggested to Lisa that she came back to my place. That way she could tell me the whole story and get herself together. She nodded, and we headed back to mine. Not far from my front door, I felt a tap on my shoulder. Liam was behind me, holding out a bag of chips. My stomach let out a happy rumble. He really was lovely, and thoughtful.

"Do you want some?" he asked Lisa, offering what was clearly his own bag of chips to her.

She turned her nose up:

"Eurgh, no way. They are way too greasy. Ever wondered why you have so many spots?" she said.

"Oi!" I snapped "no need to be such a cow. Liam is just trying to be nice".

Lisa just turned away and ignored me. I can't remember Lisa ever saying sorry for anything. While her back was turned, I grabbed Liam's hand and gave it a squeeze.

"Thanks" I said "ignore her. I'll see you later ok?"

Liam smiled, squeezed my hand back and headed off towards his house.

Lisa turned and glared at me:

"What was that all about?" she sniped.

"Nothing" I said, looking down at the pavement with embarrassment with a signature Liam-style move "He helped me study this morning and he bought me these chips so I just wanted to say thank you."

Lisa huffed and then turned and walked straight into the house. She'd been over so many times she didn't bother to knock any more.

"Is that you Ems?" my mum called through.

"Hiya, it's just Lisa and Ems" Lisa replied before I had a chance to say anything. It always amazed me how pally she was with my mother. She didn't treat her like an adult at all. If only she knew what my mother said about her when she wasn't there, then maybe she wouldn't be quite so friendly. My mother didn't have much time for Lisa. I think the phrase she used was 'a nasty piece of work'. I always used to think that was a bit harsh from my mum, but over the last few days, I'd begun to understand where she was coming from.

Lisa headed straight up to my room, just as my mother popped her head around the living room door.

"What's up with her?" she asked.

I shrugged and rolled my eyes:

"No idea. You know Lisa. She loves her drama"

My mother nodded knowingly and disappeared back to the living room.

I looked longingly at my bag of chips. We had a rule that there was no food allowed upstairs. I really wanted my chips, but I couldn't leave Lisa alone upstairs. Apart from anything else, I would sure she would nosy around my room.

Reluctantly I put my chips on the worktop in the kitchen and followed Lisa upstairs to my room. She was sat on my bed.

"Has someone else been here?" she asked, accusingly.

"Just Liam" I answered, "he came over to help me study for the maths exam tomorrow"

Lisa rolled her eyes when I mentioned Liam's name again. I let it ride because she was clearly upset. Next time, I planned to speak to her about it.

For now, Lisa had already launched into the ins and outs of her relationship with Stuart. In fairness, that was pretty normal when she came over to mine. The difference was that this time, I went through a lot of tissues. She wouldn't stop crying. It was quite hard to work out exactly what had gone on because she kept swinging between being really mean about him, and blaming herself.

As far as I could tell, Stuart had wanted to get physical with her, and she'd backed off. She said she wanted to wait but I think she was just a bit scared and didn't want to admit it. It sounded like Stuart had snapped and given her an ultimatum to have sex or stop being his girlfriend.

"He said he could have any girl he wanted" Lisa sobbed "and that all his other girlfriends had slept with him".

I was really confused (seemed to be happening a lot these days!) I could have sworn that Lisa had told me she'd slept with him already. That's why I felt that nobody liked me. Lisa was always going on about Stu and how they were made for each other. She kept telling me I had to find a boyfriend so that we could double date. I felt like such a kid compared to Lisa and her steady relationship. But now she was making it sound like a totally different relationship. Stuart just hung out with his mates all the time and he didn't seem to have much time for her at all. And it sounded like they hadn't done very much…you know…stuff…with each other.

"I really thought he was the one, you know" she stifled yet another sob "I thought I was different from all the other girls he'd been with. Everybody wanted him you know? But he chose me."

Lisa seemed to have forgotten I was in the room. She had started on a diatribe.

"I knew he loved me. He didn't have to say it. He just showed it in little ways. He would take me to clubs with him. He even got me a fake ID so I could get in with him". Remembering I was in the room too for a moment, she turned to me "Remember, he offered to get you one too? But you were too prudish and said you would prefer to stay at home".

I did remember. She wanted me to go to a club with her when I didn't even have anyone to go with. I Would feel like a total spare part. And I had no money. And I don't even like drinking. Besides, I'd been burned by Lisa's plans with Stu before. She once offered me a lift home from school only to decide to tell me last minute that Stu had changed his mind and was giving a lift to his mates, so there was no room for me. Luckily, I just managed to run to the bus as it was setting off and it was the friendly bus driver that day who stopped and let me on. I vowed then never to trust Lisa for anything like that again.

"You wouldn't understand" she continued "it's different when you are with older guys. They aren't childish like Liam and those other losers in our class."

I decided not to rise to the bait on that one. She was upset.

"Maybe that was the problem" she said, following a train of thought in her head "maybe it was you lot that put him off, hanging around me all the time and being all needy and childish".

She was starting to really annoy me. Why on earth did she bother with me if I was that childish and pathetic? Whose bed was she sitting on right now? Who had given her somewhere safe to go? Who had covered for her all those times with her dad. Did she not appreciate anything?

I had no idea what to say.

Then I remembered Caveman and Ninja. Maybe they could help me. And I really needed to get out of the room before I lost it with her.

I left her mid-sob and sat at the top of the stairs to message the guys. I figured Caveman wouldn't be much use so I messaged Ninja.

Me: Hey Ninja, what do you reckon I should say to Lisa? She either has a go at me or sobs more when I say anything.

Ninja: Everybody lies.

Me: Erm….oooh…kayy….

Ninja: Seriously, you have no idea about her relationship. You only know what she decided to tell you. And everybody sees things their own way. And then, when friends talk, they often lie to make themselves feel better. Lisa lied about the way her relationship with Stuart went. I can guarantee it.

This was not helping. What was I supposed to do, comfort her by telling her not to worry, she was a lying cow anyway. Honestly!

Ninja: Why didn't you tell her what went on with Liam?

I thought about that. Why didn't I tell her? Well, I didn't want her to make fun of me. But it was deeper than that. It was private. Between me and Liam. I didn't want her in the middle of it. I wasn't even sure myself about what was going on. She would have confused it more.

Ninja: See, you never know what's going on in someone else's head. Besides, she doesn't care what you say right now. She's too wrapped up in her own stuff. Don't worry about it. Just listen. You're a good friend.

Ninja had a point. I don't think Lisa wanted me to say anything. She just wanted somewhere that wasn't her house to hang out. I supposed the good thing was that I wouldn't have to lie about her being over at my house to her dad anymore!

I decided to go downstairs and see if I could get some chips before they went stone cold. I doubted Lisa would even notice that I'd gone.

My mum was in the kitchen eating my chips. As soon as she saw me, she wiped her hands on her jeans and turned towards the kettle as if she was making a cup of coffee. I smiled to myself. If she'd just asked, I would have happily shared my chips with her. But I knew she never would because they were 'bad for her diet'.

"What's up with little miss drama queen now?" asked my mum, glancing upstairs towards my room.

"She got dumped" I said, grabbing one of the few remaining chips from the wrapper. It was a crispy one. Everyone knows the crispy ones taste nicer. They were just on the verge of being too cold to eat. I wanted to just shove the rest of the chips in my mouth. They didn't have enough salt on them, but I didn't care. The first chip sat really heavily on my stomach.

"Surprised it took that long!" scoffed my mother.

I swallowed another chip down a little too fast, and after I'd finished trying not to choke I said "That's not very fair. But true".

I offered the bag of chips to my mother. She waved them away, but I could see her eyeing them longingly. I figured if I left some behind, she'd probably finish them off in secret. It was hard to stop when there were still some left but I was finding it hard to eat when I was aware she kept glancing over when she thought I wasn't looking. It was just like one of those dog videos you see on YouTube where the dog looks away when the human looks at them, and looks at the food whenever they turn away.

"I'm stuffed" I said, patting my stomach, "and I best get back to Lisa. Who knows what she's up to in my room".

I headed back upstairs, catching a sneaky glance into the kitchen as my mother headed straight for the chips once I was gone. I smiled to myself.

I got back to my room just in time. Lisa had clearly recovered enough from her heartache to stop crying and was now standing up, hovering over my journal. A couple more minutes and she would have read everything I'd written about her in the last couple of days. What a disaster that would have been!

"Feeling better?" I asked, pretending I didn't know what she was about to do.

She at least had the decency to look guilty.

"Erm…yeah…I'm better off without him anyway. I can do so much better than Stu. All he wanted to do was hang out with his mates. Besides, at least now I won't have to lie to my dad so much."

'Nor will I' I thought. Of course, Lisa never said thank you to me for covering her before, so why would she say it now.

Lisa was definitely re-writing her story of events. She was now unrecognisable as the person outside the chipshop with her face blotchy from crying. I was quite impressed. I wish I was that good at getting over stuff. I'd stew on things for days, sometimes even weeks. This one time, a boy had laughed when I walked past him. I must have been in the first year of high school. I had no idea why he laughed. I ran to the bathroom to see if there was anything on my face, or anything obvious. But there was nothing. Actually, come to think of it, I'm still not over that and it's 4 years later! I guess Ninja would say it was nothing to do with me. Maybe he's right.

"So, I'll just sort my make-up out and then pop over the road to get my books and we can study for the exam tomorrow" she said, digging her make-up out of her bag. Lisa never went anywhere without her make-up.

Lisa wasn't even asking if I wanted to study. She was just assuming that we would.

"Actually, I'm good. I'm all set for tomorrow" I said.

Lisa stopped halfway through putting her lipstick on and just stared at me. It was the first time since she'd come into my room that she'd paid any attention to me.

"No way." She snapped "You are rubbish at maths. You know how nervous you get before tests. You need my help to prepare. You'll fall to bits if I don't help you."

In fairness, she was right. Lisa knew what I was like with tests. It wasn't that she said anything deep and meaningful to help, it's just that she wittered on so much that it would distract me from worrying about it.

I was quite miffed with her despite this. She obviously saw me as this pathetic girl who couldn't do anything without her help. She was well overestimating what she did to help me.

"Seriously," I replied, starting to get quite upset with her for treating me like a muppet "I studied with Liam. I think I've got everything I'm gonna get"

For once, Lisa appeared lost for words. For a moment, I glimpsed the face of a hurt little girl again, until she put the façade back on and carried on with her lipstick.

"Fine" she said (although it sounded more like 'thine' because she had her mouth in a grimace while she applied lipstick) "just don't cry on my shoulder when you mess it up".

The cheek of her! And after I'd 'rescued' her off the street a few hours ago.

We didn't say a word after that. I just remained on the bed while she finished her make-up. Then she went downstairs and headed back to her house without even saying thank you, or good luck for tomorrow, or anything.

I went through to the kitchen and noticed the chip wrapper was now gone from the worktop. My mother had obviously finished them off and gone back to her Uni work.

I wandered around, wondering what I should no next. Liam was back home and I had no way of getting in touch with him. I felt like I should do some more revision, but I surprised myself when I realised I had meant what I said to Lisa. I really did feel like I was ready for my exam tomorrow.

I went into the lounge and asked mum if she fancied watching some Netflix or a movie. She looked relieved to have an excuse to take a break from her work, and quickly closed off her laptop and joined me on the sofa.

I don't think I have ever been as relaxed before a test as I was today.

It was certainly another interesting day, that's for sure!

FRIDAY: EVERYBODY LIES

I woke up today feeling fine. This may not seem like anything weird, but I have never felt fine before a test. More than anything I was looking forward to catching the bus to school, because I would get to see Liam again. Weirdly, all I could think of was Liam. I tried glancing through some of my maths stuff and felt like none of it was sticking. If I wasn't careful I was in danger of freaking myself out. I decided not to even try and look at my work and instead, I headed off to the bus stop early. I knew the bus wouldn't come any quicker, but I certainly wasn't going to risk missing it on today of all days.

My mother was still in bed, but yelled through when she heard me leave my room.

"Good luck darling, you'll be great. Don't worry. Remember to breathe!"

I laughed. Normally it would have annoyed me that she was treating me like an idiot. But today I was able to take it as a genuine sign she cared.

I thanked her and headed downstairs. I thought about breakfast and then I thought about Liam, and the chips I'd eaten yesterday. No. Now, more than ever, I needed to get control of my eating. Liam and I had only just got together. My first boyfriend. Maybe? I wasn't even sure if he was my boyfriend. Aren't you supposed to ask each other out or something? I had no idea. Normally I'd ask Lisa, but somehow, I didn't think her answer would be very helpful. Anyway, it would be the shortest relationship in history if I kept piling the weight on. No breakfast for me today. Or any day. And no lunch. I was just going to eat small dinners from now on.

When I got to the bus stop, Lisa was already there. This was unheard of. She looked a mess. She looked like she'd been crying all night.

"Don't say a word" she snapped "I don't want to hear it"

I wasn't going to say anything. I had no idea what she was talking about. She had seemed ok when she left mine last night. I wondered if her dad had found out or something. Clearly, she wasn't in the mood for talking about it, so I just dug out my phone and scrolled through to check out what I missed. I was a little distracted yesterday so hadn't really checked.

Lisa grabbed my arm, nearly knocking my phone onto the floor.

"Hey, watchit!" I yelled "You nearly made me drop my phone then!"

To my surprise, Lisa apologised. Not only did she apologise, but she started asking me questions. About me. She never asked about me. She usually just told me about herself.

Just then a car raced by revving its engine. The music was blaring and the windows were fully wound down. I could see that Stu was driving. Someone leaned out of the window and yelled

"Lisa is a prude!" so loudly that even people walking further down the street turned to look.

'Really?' I thought to myself. None of the over-sharing that Lisa had done with me made me think of her as a prude. Actually, quite the opposite. I was amazed at the stuff she said she did with Stu.

I looked at Lisa, expecting her to be laughing and full of bravado like s̷ normally was.

But she wasn't.

Her face was bright red and she was clearly trying to shrink herself in smallest size she could. Her arms were wrapped tightly around her chest and she was leaning into the corner of the bus stop (a place most of us never went near because it stank like a toilet).

She was trying not to make eye contact with anyone and tears were streaming down her face.

I felt sorry for her. I had no idea what was going on. Those lads hadn't really done anything much. They certainly didn't say anything that bad. Why wasn't she giving as good as she got like she normally did?

I reached out to reassure her, but she just shrugged my hand away violently, grabbed her bag and ran to her house. I think that was the first time since I'd known her that I'd ever seen Lisa run anywhere. She was the only person I'd ever met that always seemed to get out of P.E. God knows, I'd tried a few times myself but it never seemed to work. Whereas the teacher seemed to smile at Lisa and let her sit out whatever we were doing. She didn't even have to get changed into the stupid gym kit.

It also meant she never had to worry about showers afterwards. It amazed me how some girls didn't seem to care at all and brazenly showered without even trying to hide themselves. Then again, if my body looked anything like theirs, I probably wouldn't be as fussed about flashing it to everyone in the room. I, on the other hand, had mastered the art of sneaking in and out of the showers without actually showering. In fairness, there were some parts of gym I liked. I was on the hockey team and enjoyed that, as long as I could be in a position where I didn't have to run too much. The only problem with hockey is that you played through the winter and it was cold and wet. Netball was better because it was often indoors and the Netball court is way smaller than the Hockey field.

Lisa ran home. It appeared she was actually capable of running. I hoped that her dad was away with work because she was going to be in so much trouble if he wasn't.

I watched her front door closely, to see if she was coming back out and needed a little moral support. For a while I forgot that I was waiting for the bus. The bus eventually turned up and blocked my view of her house. There was nothing more I could do. I got on but kept watching behind me to see if she'd jump on the bus last minute. When the bus pulled away, I realised she wasn't get on it. Which would mean she'd miss her exam. She was going to be in so much trouble.

Liam was in his normal seat and on his own, as usual. I sat next to him. He looked at me with a weird look on his face. Oh god, maybe I totally misinterpreted yesterday. Maybe he didn't like me at all and was just happy to be studying with someone. I was so embarrassed. What could I do though? If I moved that would look even weirder.

I tried to avoid looking at him. I picked up my phone and messaged Ninja.

Me: Ninja, help! I got it all wrong. Liam doesn't like me. He doesn't want me to sit next to him. What should I do?

Ninja: Seriously? I mean, really. You still think you can read minds? Even after everything I've said?

Me: No need to be like that. It's pretty obvious. He just gave me a weird look.

Ninja: A weird look? Hmm let's think, what other possible reasons could there be for a 'weird' look?

I got the sense that Ninja was being sarcastic with me. However, I had asked for his help, so it would be pretty stupid to ignore what he was saying.

I looked again at Liam. He was no longer looking at me and had returned to picking at the thread on his rucksack. Although now, he pulled the thread away from his body. He'd clearly learned from smacking himself in the face. I smiled when I remembered that. He'd looked so silly. And then I remembered the photo Lisa had taken and stopped smiling. Was that really only a few days ago? How could I possible smile at any part of that memory. As I already said, I was the master at stewing on stuff.

ping

Ninja: The way you remember stuff changes all the time. Every time you learn something new, it changes the way a memory is stored. Because you now think of Liam with fondness, you can smile at that memory, rather than only remembering your embarrassment.

I was embarrassed now. Ninja said I was fond of Liam. What if Liam was looking over my shoulder and read that? I glanced across at him nervously. No need to worry. He was still focussed on that same thread.

"So..erm…where is Lisa today?" he asked, clearly trying to sound unconcerned.

"No idea" I answered, glad to have someone to share what had happened with. "It was really weird. She was at the bus stop. Early. Lisa is NEVER early. And these lads drove past, said some stuff and then she ran home."

"So she's gonna miss the exam?" Liam asked, surprising me by showing genuine concern for a girl that had been nothing but mean to him. Then again, I reminded myself that I was friends with that girl and had joined in most of the time. I felt bad. Why was Liam even talking to me?

I nodded. Distracted.

"Ah" he said as if suddenly realising something "that's why you sat next to me. I thought you'd be too embarrassed to be seen with me if Lisa was around".

He was right of course.

Liam had been way nicer to me in the last few days than Lisa had been in all the time I'd known her, and yet I knew I still cared what she thought. I was so shallow.

ping

I looked at my phone because I really didn't know how to answer that.

Ninja: Sooooo…that 'weird' look, what could it have possibly been about?

I growled at my phone, switched it to silent and shoved it in my bag.

Liam gave me another weird look but this time I knew it was about the phone.

"I'm worried it will go off in the exams". Well it was only half a lie. I really didn't want it to go off in the exams. It's just not necessarily the reason I had switched it off just then.

Once I stopped worrying what Liam thought of me, I settled down to the bus trip to school. I looked around the bus at the other kids. It wasn't something I usually paid much attention to. I was too busy worrying what everyone else thought of me. Today was a bit different though. I found that I was curious about what everyone else was up to.

I noticed that quite a lot of them were focussed on their phones. I guess there was nothing unusual in that. The unusual thing was they seemed to be pointing at something and laughing and then sharing it with the person next to them.

Clearly someone was being humiliated again. For a very brief moment I panicked thinking it might have been something else about me, but no one seemed to be glancing in my direction. Besides, I hadn't really done anything that I could think of that was worthy of sharing for a laugh.

There was a little niggle at the back of my mind though, that it might be something I wanted to learn about. I dismissed the thought. I had too much to worry about with my upcoming exam to give any space to what was going on with anyone else. At least, for now anyway.

Liam and I spent the rest of the journey to school testing each other on our Maths knowledge. There were a couple of things where I panicked and had to look them up but generally was ok until we were waiting outside the room to go in and take the exam.

I started feeling that familiar sickness. I was quite glad I hadn't eaten breakfast because I thought I was going to be sick. I also felt light headed. It was like everything I had learnt had vanished from my head. Liam tried to talk to me but I couldn't respond. I felt breathing rapidly was the only thing stopping me barfing right then.

Maybe Lisa was right. Maybe I needed her. Then again, when I thought about it, I still freaked out just as much whether Lisa was there or not. It's just that I was more distracted.

Liam was still talking.

"I panic about exams too" he was saying.

This registered. Him? There was no way he was panicking.

"No way" I said. Turns out, Liam could also be a distraction.

"Yes way" he said, smiling at his own joke.

"When I was little and freaking out about everything, my mum wasn't as ill. She would spend a lot of time with me, helping me deal with stuff". Liam stopped for a moment. He looked like a hurt puppy again. Before I could say anything, he carried on, "She taught me a trick where I sing a song and did a counting thing to help me cope. It worked really well. I still do it now" He looked at the floor for a moment "I even did it yesterday when we you know…erm" and he looked around "…nearly…thing" he whispered as his voice trailed off.

It was a shame my mother had come into the room. I really wanted to kiss Liam. I blushed at the thought, and to recover from the moment I said:

"I don't think I can sing a song". I tried hard not to lose track of my breathing as I spoke. It was close. I was nearly sick. Barfing on Liam would not have been good form at this early stage of our…our what? Relationship? That seemed a bit strong. Friendship? No, it was more than that.

"Well" Liam smiled "It's pretty easy. I was only 8 when she taught it to me after all. Besides, you don't sing out loud. You just play the music in your head with an imaginary play button."

That sounded like I might be able to do it.

"So here's what you do: You count your breathing. You breathe in and count to 2, then out and count to 2. You breathe in and count to 3, and out and count to 3. And you keep going increasing by one until you get to 10. Then you start again at 2"

I was trying, but it was tricky. I was getting as far as 4 and feeling like I was going to explode.

"I can't get past 4" I gasped, letting out a lung full of air.

"That's ok" said Liam supportively, "you just go as high as you can then back to 2. You don't have to get to 10 at first"

He really was good at this teaching thing. I felt quite proud of him. Then I realised how weird that was and concentrated on my breathing again. I could just about manage to get up to 6 before I felt like I was gonna explode.

"Right, good. Next…" he said.

"Wait, there's more? Seriously?" I gasped.

Liam smiled.

"The breathing bit is good distraction for your body" he explained "but you also need to distract your brain. This is where the song comes in. So, think of a song"

I was struggling to think of anything right then other than not running out of breath and dying.

"You got one?" he asked.

"No" I puffed "I can't think at all right now"

"Ok how about a song that makes you dance round your room?"

How did he know I danced around my room to music? Did he have a hidden camera or something?

Liam smiled and continued "We all have a song that makes us feel like dancing don't we?"

Phew. No hidden camera. He was just assuming something. He was right too. I definitely had a song I could think of that I loved to dance to (on my own in my room!).

"Yeah sure" I said.

"Right, now imagine pressing play on that song and then whacking the volume up full blast. But, you gotta keep doing the breathing thing at the same time" he said.

"What? I can't breathe and sing! I'll collapse"

The weird thing was, I had already forgotten about my nerves. I couldn't panic about an exam and do a stupid breathing thing and play a song in my head at the same time.

I concentrated on my song and the breathing. It was tricky but I was just kind of getting it when, to my surprise, we were called into the room for the exam. I'd totally forgotten about that. How had I forgotten about an exam when I was stood right outside ready to go in and take it?

Once we were all sat down I glanced around the room while I waited for them to tell us we could turn our papers over. I noticed Lisa sat on the far side of the room by the door. She must have got a lift in with her mum and snuck in after the rest of us. I was glad she made it, and I was curious to learn what was going on. But for now, I needed to focus on the exam.

Just then, my stomach rumbled so loudly that, due to the room being in exam conditions, everybody in the room heard it, and a few people even sniggered.

I was just about to worry about what they thought, when the teacher told us that it was ok to start the exam.

I hate that moment. The moment where you first see the exam paper and see the questions you will have to answer. I have this fear that I will read them and not be able to answer any of them. I try and find the question that I know well and answer that first. Somehow, this time, there were loads of different questions I could easily pick from to answer first.

I felt myself relaxing into the questions. I kept reading and re-reading each question to make sure I didn't make any stupid mistakes. I even checked each answer at least once.

Even so, I'd finished the exam with half an hour still to spare and now had nothing else to do.

By now my stomach was constantly rumbling and I was even constantly feeling light headed. I wished I'd eaten some breakfast. I tried to look around surreptitiously. Both Liam and Lisa still had their heads down, scribbling away. In fact, I seemed to be the only one that had finished. The good thing was, everyone was now so focussed on their exams that they didn't notice my stomach rumbling any more.

I panicked for a moment. Maybe I'd missed a side of the paper. I looked through it again, but, no, I'd definitely answered every question.

I didn't want it to be obvious that I'd finished so I started messing with my calculator and drawing on my pencil case. It was going to be a very long half an hour. And I had a very small pencil case!

About 10 minutes before the end of the exam (and after what felt like hours of messing with my calculator), Liam put his pen down and glanced over at me. He smiled. I shrugged and yawned. We then proceeded to have a whole conversation in gestures, occasionally glancing at the teacher to make sure they didn't notice. As we got closer to the finish time, the noise in the room began to subtly increase, as more people finished.

Lisa was still writing. I had noticed a panicked look on her face when the teacher gave the 15-minute warning and she'd been frantically writing ever since. It was weird because I wasn't sure how you could actually do that much writing in a maths exam.

Finally, the teacher told us to put our pens down and I heard a collective sigh of relief from the room. Well, except for Lisa who let out a panicked sounding squeal that made quite a few people turn and look at her. I felt sorry for her. I knew that feeling. Somehow, this exam was fine. In fact, it was very different from any exam/test I'd taken before. I did my best, and I knew that's all I could do. Besides, the results didn't really matter. Well, to me anyway. To Liam, who was trying to prove his dad wrong, it was super important. And to Lisa who had all that pressure from her dad to study law, every single test was important. To her dad, even if not to her.

I planned to catch up with her after. Something was definitely going on. Unfortunately, because she was close to the door, she was first out of the room. Still, I expected to find her waiting outside for our normal post-exam debrief, but when I eventually got out, there was no sign of her.

I switched my phone off silent and checked for messages, thinking maybe she'd got fed up of waiting and had messaged me to meet somewhere.

Nothing.

I decided to check Facebook. In all honesty, I hadn't wanted to look at it since all that stuff at the start of the week, but I was feeling ok now. Sod them. I didn't care what everyone else thought.

The first thing I saw was a video of Lisa. It looked like someone had sneaked into a room she was in while she was getting changed. I'd never actually been to her house, so I didn't know if it was her room. Although I doubted it, as there is no way she would risk someone in her house. Also, the room looked very masculine. There were pictures of footballers and cars around the room, and an Xbox and a giant TV on the far side of Lisa.

The person videoing it could be heard breathing heavily. You could see a blurry reflection of the person holding the camera in the TV. You could also see a reflection of Lisa but the light was such that you couldn't make out much. Lisa initially had her back to the camera. You could see her lift her shirt over her head and see her bra, mainly from the back, but a little from the front as she turned when she folded her shirt and put it on the bed next to her. When she went to put her shirt down, she saw the person in the doorway.

"Stu!" she screamed and picked up a nearby pillow and threw it at him. It knocked the phone out of his hand and the screen went black.

"Oi, you mad cow!" Stu yelled back. "You are such a prude. Go home. This is no place for little girls."

Then you could hear a rustling and brief view of Stu's grinning face, before the video was stopped.

No wonder Lisa was a mess. I don't think I would have even left the house if I knew that was all over Facebook. It certainly explained those lads in the car this morning, and why Lisa had run home after.

It was also obviously what everyone was looking at on the bus. I looked at the numbers on the video. Wow, it had been viewed over 600 times and been shared 123 times. It had gone viral. Anyone who had Facebook would pretty much have seen it by now.

"Wait, was that Lisa? No wonder she's upset." Liam made me jump. Speaking of someone who wasn't on Facebook, he'd been as clueless as me over what was upsetting Lisa. He must have been one of the only kids in the school that didn't use social media.

"What a scumbag her boyfriend is. Why would you do that to someone?" he asked.

I shook my head. I had no idea. I had thought they were in love. Certainly, from everything Lisa talked about. Although, now I thought about it, she had mentioned a few times how Stu wanted her to go a bit further with him and she'd told him that she wasn't ready. She said he was really sweet about it. Obviously, that was only to her face. It was clearly a different story when her back was turned.

Something else suddenly came to mind that now made a lot of sense.

A few months ago, I'd been out with my mum food shopping (that's a whole other story!) when I could have sworn I saw Stuart snogging a girl. There was no way it was Lisa. This girl was tall and skinny and had blonde hair. Lisa had dark hair. I thought maybe it was just someone that looked like Stuart. Later that night, Lisa was round at my house, when I told her how I'd seen a guy that looked exactly like Stu, but no way it could have been him because he was snogging another girl.

For a moment, Lisa's face had looked like thunder, until the standard fake smile reappeared and she said "You are so silly. There is only one Stuart and he is definitely mine!"

I thought nothing of it and left it there. But now I look back, it probably was him I saw. He obviously had a very different view of the relationship than Lisa. What was it Ninja said? Everybody lies about their relationships.

I wanted to message Lisa to ask if she was ok. Of course, she wouldn't be. What would I even say to her? She probably would keep her phone switched off at the moment anyway. I certainly would if I was her. In fact, I did at the start of the week. Not that what had happened to me was anywhere near as bad as this video. It put things into perspective a little.

My stomach rumbled again.

I had been totally lost there for a while, but my stomach brought me back to reality.

"So, what did you think of the exam?" I asked Liam.

"Awful" Liam replied, "I'll be lucky if I scraped a pass"

I said nothing. It was usually me saying that and Lisa telling me she'd found it easy. I used to hate it when she did that! Mind you, we'd often get similar marks when the results came out.

Everybody lies.

"I'm sure you did better than you think" I tried to reassure him. He always aced tests. He was the only kid in the class that ever got 100% on things. It was weird hearing him say he thought he had done badly on the exam. I wondered if he was just saying it to make me feel better. I didn't think that Liam would do that. Then again, I really didn't know him that well at all. I bet Lisa thought she knew Stu until he posted that stuff.

"Yeah, well let's forget about it, shall we?" I nudged Liam, "remember, we've still got the fun of more exams next week."

Liam groaned.

I groaned inside too, but not at the thought of the other exams. It was the realisation that this was the only subject Liam and I shared, so there would be no excuse to study together again for a while.

As if reading my mind Liam said "We can still study together even though we don't share subjects. Maybe we can quiz each other and stuff?"

"Ok" I said. I tried to appear indifferent. Lisa had always said that you should not appear too keen to boys because it would put them off you. Then I remembered the video and the lies, and decided I needed to be a little clearer with Liam.

"That's a really good idea. I enjoyed spending time with you these last couple of days"

"Me too" said Liam as he reached for my hand and gave it a little squeeze. I felt my heart race. At first I thought it was because I was worried what everyone would thing, and glanced round nervously.

Then I realised it was a happy heart racing. I had a boyfriend. Me. Of all people and after all this time. I actually had a boyfriend. And Lisa had nothing to do with it. Well almost nothing. If she hadn't shared that stupid picture, he would never have walked me home and then this would never have happened. I wasn't going to thank her though!

My stomach rumbled again.

Dammit! Why would it not just shut up. I really wanted to skip lunch today. Especially now with Liam and stuff. God, can you imagine what would happen if someone videoed me and saw all those rolls of fat around my middle. I physically shuddered when I thought of it.

"Want to get some lunch?" Liam asked.

"Don't take this the wrong way, but I think I best go find Lisa" I lied "you go and get yourself something and I'll see you on the bus."

The exam was over and we had nothing more to do, but it wasn't easy to get home so I was stuck with waiting around for the bus at the end of the day.

Luckily Liam understood. He even asked me to give his best wishes to Lisa when I saw her. I told him I would, but there was no way I was going to say anything about Liam to Lisa. Besides, she probably wouldn't even let me get a word in, knowing her.

I wasn't totally sure where she'd be, but I did have a few places to look. Lisa liked to smoke, but only usually when she was with the boys. I was always a bit jealous of how good she was at fitting in. I really wanted to smoke too, but I knew my mother would go spare if she smelt even a hint of smoke on me. My grandmother and auntie both died of breast cancer. My mother said we had the markers in our family for it. She'd even had a double mastectomy to make sure that she didn't get it. I think that's part of the reason she was always so down on the way she looked.

So I tried to avoid hanging out with the smokers. I didn't want to upset my mum.

The advantage of being just out of an exam was that most of the school was still in lessons, so the corridors and school grounds were clear of kids.

Lisa was in the second place I looked; a sheltered annex at the end of the school building.

She glanced at me as I approached, but didn't say a thing. She took another drag of her cigarette. I was going to have to take a risk if I was going to talk to her, and get close enough to get the smell of cigarettes on my clothes. In fact, I would probably tell my mother what I did before she even asked and got me into trouble.

"I saw the video" I said.

Lisa said nothing. She just took another drag on the cigarette.

"Wanna talk about it?"

She shook her head.

We stood there in silence for a while.

"You know," I said "this guy...well a friend...once told me, everybody lies. Especially about relationships."

I waited a moment then continued.

"You know that time I said I saw someone that looked like Stuart?"

I waited for an answer. She said nothing.

"That was actually Stu wasn't it?"

She still said nothing. But a tear rolled down her cheek and landed on her cigarette with a hiss.

She threw it to the ground and stomped it out, grinding it up so no one else could use it.

"Oh Ems," she sobbed "I'm such an idiot. Why would he do that to me?

He said he loves me"

"Everybody lies" I answered.

"But not us. We had something special. I know it."

"What's this all really about?" I asked. I could see that Lisa wasn't just trying to lie to me, she was lying to herself. For a moment I thought about just walking away. But she was my friend and she was hurting. I really believed I could help her. Ok, it may be the stuff that Ninja and Caveman had said that I was repeating, but still, it was true. Maybe it would help her to see things differently.

"You wouldn't understand" she snapped "you don't know what it's like to be in a proper relationship."

She was right of course. Although I suspected my 'relationship' with Liam over the last couple of days was far more honest than the one she'd had with Stuart had ever been.

She always said things that hurt. I took a deep breath and reminded myself that this wasn't about me. It was about her.

"Try me" I said.

She reached into her back and took out a packet of cigarettes, reached in, took another one out and lit it.

She blew the smoke away, pointing her lips slightly upwards. It was a posed I recognised. I'd seen her mother do the same.

She seemed to decide to talk to me.

For the next hour or so, Lisa told me everything that had happened. She told me what she was doing in Stu's bedroom.

It had started with him wanting to take pictures of her with no clothes on. At first she'd refused, but he made her feel like she wasn't mature enough for him, so she had caved and let him take them.

A week or so later, she had caught him showing the pictures to his friends.

She went mad at him. He just laughed and said he wanted to show off his gorgeous girlfriend. She was flattered by this, even though it made her uncomfortable so she said nothing more. She made him promise not to ever share them online. He said he'd never do that to her.

Then he started wanting to do more than kiss. At first she let him put his hand down her top but then when he wanted more she started pulling away. That's when he first called her a prude. He said all the other girls that he'd been with went a lot further than that. He suggested she was too young. Apparently, that was around the same time that I saw him kissing the other girl. Because of what I told her, she decided that the only way she was going to keep Stu was to do more with him.

It was never enough though. He kept threatening to dump her for someone that was more mature and would sleep with him. She was worried what everyone would think, so she eventually decided to do it.

The video was the night she was going to sleep with him. She was in his room. He said she should get undressed while he went and fetched a condom. He left her in his room, pretending to give her some privacy. At first she got cold feet and decided to tell him she wouldn't sleep with him. But then, after he'd been gone a while, she worried what he would tell his friends. She thought maybe he would share the photos he'd taken of her. She started to get undressed and noticed him in the doorway. She went mad at him (as we all now knew) put her clothes back on and left.

He started sending her nasty messages pretty much straight away. "Prude" and "Immature" were nothing compared to the other things he said about her.

Then he shared that video.

"And now everyone knows I'm a prude. I'll never get a boyfriend again" she sobbed.

Seriously? I couldn't believe that out of everything she'd just told me, the thing that was really upsetting her was that other boys would think she was a prude.

"But actually, I don't want another boyfriend"

'Phew' I thought.

Then her lip wobbled and another tear rolled down her cheek.

"I want Stu. I love him"

All hope was lost. How could she want to be with him after the way he had treated her? I didn't get it.

I took out my phone to ask Ninja what to do. Lisa went spare at me.

"You're looking at it again aren't you? That stupid video. You're just like everybody else. I thought you were my friend Ems!" she yelled, and then, throwing yet another cigarette to the ground, she grabbed her bagged and stormed off. I was left with my mouth hanging open. I didn't even have a chance to say a word.

ping

Ninja: When I said everybody lies, it includes lying to themselves.

Me: But why doesn't she see how horrible Stuart is being? Surely it's obvious?

Caveman: Pick me, pick me!

I smiled. I wondered what Caveman could really add.

Me: Ok go on then...

Caveman: We all need to be liked and loved. To fit in. Lisa needs to be liked and needs to believe she it. The idea that she got it wrong, and is not liked, is just too significant to process, so she chooses not to believe it.

Ninja: He's actually right. If you can learn to not care what people think (because you can't ever know) then you can enjoy life a lot more. Nobody really fits in. We are all different.

Ninja: And boys are stupid. They only care about sex. They are as primitive as caveman. Girls build things up in their heads. They want romance and love. Boys want a shag. It's a bit of a problem really.

Caveman: Oi! I resent that. I am not stupid! Well, not very. Ok well I am a bit primitive but only because I want to stop you dying! *humpf*

I thought about what had happened with Lisa. I thought about Liam, and how wrong I was about him. Then I thought about Stuart and his mates. They were always making fun of others, including each other. They did seem to think of girls as conquests. I had never liked Stu or any of his friends, despite Lisa's attempts to set me up with at least 3 of them.

Lisa was different when she was around them. She always used to criticise people, but she was a lot nastier around Stu. It seemed the only way she could feel good about herself was to make other people feel rubbish.

I felt sorry for her. It mattered so much what other people thought of her.

It was at this point I stopped for a moment with a weird and freaky realisation.

I felt sorry for Lisa. I had never felt sorry for her before. I had spent most of our friendship trying to live up to her expectations of me. But I realised now that I didn't care what she thought of me. She was totally screwed up. I wouldn't swap my life for hers for any amount of money.

Wow! That was gonna take some thinking about.

I looked at my watch. Not long until the bus. I didn't fancy trying to talk to Lisa again, and, at that moment, I didn't really fancy talking to Liam. So I took a walk over to where the buses were. I pulled up my phone and looked through Facebook for a while. I checked out some of the comments on Stuart's post. Who were those people who said such vile things? They didn't even know Lisa. What made them think it was ok to say things like that about somebody else.

I shuddered. Imagine if it was me. From what Lisa described, it easily could have been. I decided to do something unusually bold for me, I reported the post to Facebook. I knew they were pretty strict about nudity and stuff because my mother once ranted on for days about a post of hers they deleted. It was something to do with breast cancer. She'd shared a photo of someone who had a similar operation to hers, and someone had reported it. Facebook had removed the photo within a day. My mum was fuming. Not so much at Facebook, but at whoever it was that had reported her. She had no idea though. That's why I felt ok with reporting it now. No one would know it was me.

There was no sign of Liam or Lisa when the bus arrived. It was weird being on the bus on my own, but I quite liked it. I listened to music and thought about some of the stuff that had happened over the last few days.

When I got in the door, my mother asked me how it had gone. I shrugged and said what I always did. I always told her it had gone ok. You really couldn't tell until the results were out, and I knew she wasn't that fussed about my results anyway.

I remembered the smoking. I thought of talking to my mum about what had happened, but she seemed to be working on something on her laptop, so I figured I would just head upstairs and get changed before she noticed.

I felt weak and lightheaded. It had been a really long day. I was passed the point of feeling hungry so decided to just have a lie down on my bed for a while. Tomorrow is the weekend and I don't need to think about exams, Lisa or anything else for a couple of days.

SATURDAY: NOT GOOD ENOUGH

The phone rang. Not my mobile. It was the home phone. Our home phone never rang. Well almost never. Sometimes you got those phone calls where they said you'd recently been in an accident. At one point we got a few of those a day. It got so annoying that we came up with a competition to see who could get rid of them quickest. My mum decided that she would begin sobbing and tell them how someone had died in the accident and how upset she was. I wasn't as good at acting as my mother, so I started accusing them of spying on me. I'd ask them how they knew. I'd suggest they were spying on me. I'd ask them for their personal details to pass on to the police. It made the calls way more fun. Eventually they stopped calling, weirdly!

At first I had no idea what the noise was. I thought it was an alarm or something. Then I heard my mum talking. She was raising her voice. This was really unusual for her. For all her issues, my mother was pretty chilled out.

I looked at the clock. 9am. I normally wouldn't get out of bed until at least 12 on a Saturday.

I couldn't make out most of what she was saying so I got out of bed and opened my door a bit to listen.

"…no…I won't let you…it's not fair on her…"

Who on earth was she talking to? Was she talking about me?

My mother went quite for a minute. Then, when she talked again, she had lowered her voice. I think she'd rumbled me. I went back to my bed. I was going to pretend not to have heard it. Hopefully she would tell me what was going on when she got off the phone.

A few minutes later, I heard her coming up the stairs.

"Ems, are you awake?" She called as she gently knocked on my bedroom door.

I feigned grogginess.

"Wassup? It's early"

"Can I come in?" she asked.

I grunted that it was ok and she came into my room.

Her eyes were red like she'd been crying. She sat on the edge of my bed and stroked my hair like she used to when I was little.

I gotta say it was quite worrying. I was trying to think of any relatives that I knew of that might have died or something. Thing was, we didn't have much family. Most of the time it was just me and my mum, and her friends. It was one of the things that I'd always been jealous about with Lisa. She had a huge family. As well as her 2two younger brothers, she had loads of uncles, aunties and cousins. And her grandparents even lived on the next street. She was always staying over with them. It gave her a break from her brothers as the house her grandparents lived in only had one small spare room. There was talk of her going to live with them when she went to Uni. Another thing I was jealous of her for. I know it's a couple of years off yet, but I have been looking at the cost of going to Uni and I don't think there is any way I can afford to stay in halls. I don't want to live at home though. That would be really sad.

Mind you, I'm not sure my mum will let me live at home. She keeps telling me to pick a Uni that is far away so I can 'experience' it. Of course, she then goes on (again!) about how she wishes she'd done that instead of having me. Yeah, yeah. Heard it all before.

Anyway, I couldn't think of anyone.

"What's up mum?" I asked.

"Your dad is coming over later to take you out for the day"

My heart was now beating as if dancing to the beat of thrash metal.

"Wait…what…my dad?"

My mother nodded.

"My actual dad?"

My mother nodded again.

"Yes, your dad. He says he'll be here in an hour. Or so." And then she muttered "if he bothers showing up"

Part of me wanted to say that I wouldn't see him. But that part wasn't loud enough to drown out the other part of me. That part was an excited 3 year old who was desperate to see her daddy again. That part was definitely winning.

I needed to get ready. I only had an hour. I tried to shove my mother out of the room.

"What's the rush?" she asked "you know he'll be late. If he turns up at all. I don't want you to get hurt. Again"

"Muuum! I only have an hour. Get out!"

My mother reluctantly left the room. What was I going to wear? I hadn't seen my dad in so long, I didn't want him to be disappointed in me. I wished I had some way of telling Liam. I really wanted to share this with someone.

I grabbed my phone to message Lisa. Dammit. I had forgotten to plug it in last night. No battery. Ah well, at least it would mean I wouldn't have to put up with annoying WhatsApp messages either. I was sure they would have something to say over this situation.

I plugged my phone in to try and give it a bit of a charge before I headed out. Even though it was my dad, from everything my mum had told me, I needed to be prepared to be left stranded somewhere.

I didn't get it. My mother told me he didn't care about me. Why would he get in touch if he didn't care.

I spent the next hour panicking about getting ready. My mother offered me breakfast but I was too nervous to eat. That was a good thing, obviously. Made the diet a lot easier to stick to.

At around 10am I went downstairs to wait. I sat near the window. I couldn't remember what he looked like. What if some stranger like the postman knocked on the door? How would I know if it was my dad.

My mother was cleaning the kitchen. She wasn't usually one for cleaning, but when she was stressed (or trying to avoid Uni work!) she cleaned. She was telling me off for everything. I didn't put stuff in the bin. I didn't put stuff in the right recycling bin. I didn't clear up my dishes. The carpet was a mess. I never helped around the house. And so on…I tuned her out. I watched out of the window. Just like I had when I was 3.

10am came and went. As did 11am. And 12. I was getting desperate for the toilet, but I knew if I went he would turn up. I wanted to see him first. I didn't want him to see my mother's miserable face.

It was no good. I had to go. After all, I didn't want to go out with him needing the loo and I wouldn't want to dash off as soon as he arrived. My mother had been rolling her eyes and huffing for the last hour. As I headed for the stairs she took my arm.

"Look Ems, don't get your hopes up ok? Even if he doesn't turn up though, we'll do something later yeah? Maybe we can go and get you new clothes or something?"

I pulled my arm away, a little more aggressively than I planned to, but she

Who was she to tell me he wasn't going to turn up. He'd called hadn't he? And the last thing I wanted to do was go clothes shopping right now. I hate clothes shopping. Everything makes me look so fat. My mum goes on about choosing a bigger size that fits better. I would die before I buy bigger size clothes. She also tries to make me try stuff on. I hate that too. I just get so depressed clothes shopping. If my mum cared about me at all, she'd know that.

"I'm going to the toilet." I snapped "If dad arrives, be nice!"

Sure enough, the doorbell went just as I sat on the toilet. I really tried to hear what was going on but it was impossible. Even worse, I was so desperate to go that I was sat there for what felt like forever. Ever had that? When you go to the toilet when you are desperate and it lasts forever?

Well, eventually it ended and I adjusted my makeup and straightened myself up a bit to make sure I looked my best (and made sure I didn't have toilet roll stuck to my bum). I was nervous. Really scared actually. What if my dad didn't like me?

I remembered I'd left my phone charging so went and grabbed that before I headed downstairs.

There was a WhatsApp message waiting for me.

Ninja: If your dad loves you, he loves you whatever. If your dad doesn't love you, he doesn't love you whatever. It's not about you.

What? Honestly, those guys made no sense whatsoever. Of course, I can make a difference. If I'm really horrible he's not going to want to see me again is he?

I was shaking so much I dropped my phone. Luckily it landed on the bed. I had a quick check for messages from Lisa but there was nothing. It was too late now to tell her about my dad so I just locked it and stuck it in my pocket.

Thinking about Lisa reminded me of the exam, and the technique Liam taught me for my nerves.

I spent a minute breathing and playing the song. I even wiggled my shoulders a bit in a dance, and then suddenly became self-conscious and paranoid that someone was watching, so stopped.

"Right, let's do this" I muttered to myself and headed downstairs.

There was no noise at all coming from the lounge. For a moment, I panicked thinking it wasn't actually him at the door. Or worse, it was him but he'd got fed up of waiting and left again. As I approached the doorway I could see a man sitting in the lounge. I could only see the side of his face. His hair was grey and his skin looked pale. He had wrinkles. Way more than my mother. I wondered how much older than her he was and why I'd never asked her that before. I really didn't know much about him. He was a stranger, sitting in my living room, about to take me out for the day.

And yet, there was a something slightly familiar about him. Maybe it was a smell, or the style of his hair. I recognised something. I felt like a 3-year-old again, standing in the doorway, too shy to go in.

My mum spotted me first.

"Ah here she is. Ems, your dad says he's really sorry but he caught in traffic." My mum had her special voice on. The one which she used when I was lying but she was waiting for me to fess up.

The strange man turned to look at me.

"Hi Emma" he said, "Like your mum says, I would have been earlier but the traffic was awful"

I wanted to believe him. I really did. But I knew it was a Saturday and traffic would not account for him being 2 hours late. I wasn't going to say anything though. Even if I wanted to say something, I was too scared. This was a weird situation.

As he had turned, I'd spotted a pink fluffy unicorn on his lap. It had a big sparkly ribbon around its neck. He saw me looking and stood up, presenting me with the unicorn.

"I got this for you" he said handing it to me. I took it. What the hell was I supposed to do with a pink fluffy unicorn? How old did he think I was? I just looked at it, lost for words. He went to hug me. I stepped back.

I couldn't help it. It was an involuntary reaction as a result of a strange bloke trying to grab me. He looked hurt. I felt bad. This was not how I imagined this scene to go when I played it through in my head. And I'd played it through a lot over the years!

He moved his hands back to his side and wiped them on his jeans, as if that's what he planned to do all along.

"Right, we best get going then" he said nervously, before asking "do you need to go to the toilet before we head off?"

I could practically hear my mother roll her eyes. This guy must have thought I was about 8 years old or something.

"Erm...no...I'm good thanks" I said, "I've just been actually."

TMI Ems. TMI.

It seemed to make him happy though. He grabbed his keys off the table and gestured me towards the front door. I automatically headed where he pointed. Just as I was heading out the door my mum called to me:

"Ems! You might want to leave the unicorn behind!"

Ah. I'd forgotten that. I couldn't believe I was about to be seen out in public carrying a pink fluffy unicorn. I asked my dad to wait a second (it feels so weird to write that), dashed upstairs, flung the pink thing on my bed, and dashed back down again.

My dad had obviously decided not to wait for me, and was now sat in a car on the street outside my house. The car didn't look like anything special. It was about 10 years old from the registration and didn't look particularly well looked after. There were various dents and scrapes in the paintwork.

Just then I spotted Lisa crossing the road and heading towards me.

Typical. Why did she choose now to decide to talk to me?

"Hi Ems" she shouted. As she got closer, she just started talking, as usual.

"I thought we could hang out today? My dad gave me some money for working hard and studying. I thought we could go into town and go clothes shopping. Stu hated clothes shopping so there is no way he'd be there. I can even spend some of it on you."

Firstly, why did everyone think I liked clothes shopping? It seemed like nobody actually knew me. Secondly, as usual, Lisa didn't let me get a word in edgeways and assumed I would drop everything and do whatever she wanted.

"I can't" I said.

"Why not?" she asked accusingly, "You're obviously not doing anything because you're heading out of the house on your own."

"Actually, I'm going out with my dad" I answered. The cheek of her.

Lisa laughed.

"Ha! Good one Ems. Next time, try a more convincing lie"

I nodded my head towards the man sat in the car, who was now looking quite impatient. When he saw I was talking to someone, he lost the grumpy look and smiled and waved.

"Seriously? That's your dad? Wow! That's a bit of a turn up for the books. Alright, well I guess I'll come with you guys and make sure you're ok then yeah?"

I could not believe the cheek of her. I hadn't seen my dad for 12 years and she thought it was ok to gatecrash our first trip out together. No way!

"Erm..no Lisa. This is my time with my dad who I've not seen in forever."

"Oh…right…I guess I'll…erm…head home then." Lisa looked hurt. She would probably be online complaining about me later but right then I didn't care. I didn't want my dad to get fed up and leave.

I ignored Lisa's sulking face and went to get in the passenger side of the car. The door was locked. My dad looked flustered for a second and leant over and unlocked it. There was a load of paperwork on the seat. He rapidly swept it off.

"Sorry" he muttered "I thought you'd sit in the back."

I looked in the back of the car. It was only a little bit clearer than the front. There was a booster seat on one of the seats.

A booster seat? I know it had been a while, but seriously?! How old did he think I was?

"Sorry. There you go" he gestured at the seat which had now been cleared by shoving all the paper to the floor. They joined the empty McDonalds coffee cups and cup holders. I awkwardly kicked stuff out of the way as I tried to get into the seat.

My father at least had the decency to look embarrassed.

I was going to make a joke and make him feel better, when it occurred to me that I didn't know what to call him. It didn't feel right to call him dad. I'm finding it weird to even write 'dad' in this diary. Then again, only really pretentious people called their parents by their first name. Besides, I realised I didn't even know his name.

This could be awkward. I decided not to decide. I could probably get away with not calling him anything.

"So where we going?" I asked, trying to break the awkward silence that seemed to be building.

"I thought we could go to McDonalds for lunch" he said, "my treat obviously".

McDonalds! Was he kidding me? I didn't see him for 12 years and when I did he brought me a kids toy, thought I was going to sit in a booster seat and figured lunch in McDonalds was a treat! Who was this guy? And the worst thing was, I was going to have to eat. If I didn't eat something he would get all upset and think he'd done something wrong. Or maybe he'd ask me why and I'd have to explain. Oh God, this was turning out to be the worst day ever.

I shrugged. I really didn't know what to say. I forgot he was driving, so couldn't see.

"Is that not ok?" he asked. I was sure he sounded a little cross. I was messing this up good and proper.

"Oh no, it's fine" I rapidly answered, trying to sound as enthusiastic as I could.

McDonalds wasn't even that far away. I wondered if I could get away with just having a drink or if he would notice and get offended. I giggled to myself when I realised he'd probably just offer me a Happy Meal. Good thing about that was that a Happy Meal is at least a really small portion and wouldn't blow my diet too much. I secretly quite like the toys too. Especially the Minions. They were great.

Thinking about The Minions gave me an idea.

"Hey…" and then an awkward silence because I couldn't work out what to call him "…maybe we could go to the cinema?"

It seemed like a really good idea to me. We wouldn't have to talk but we could spend time together. And I wouldn't have to eat anything.

My dad looked uncomfortable.

"The cinema is quite expensive sweetie. Maybe another time"

Sweetie? I guess he couldn't remember my name either then eh?

I felt like telling him he could spend some of the money he'd saved by not buying me birthday presents for the last 12 years, but thought better of it.

This had gone from being something I was excited about, to something I just needed to get through. I wished I'd said yes to Lisa.

We got to McDonalds in no time at all. We parked up and went in. I looked around, scanning faces for anyone I knew. I was getting ready to hide my face if I spotted someone.

And then I felt my heart jump. Over in the corner, on his own, huddled over a Happy Meal, was Liam. He didn't recognise me at first. He must have seen my dad and assumed it was someone who just looked like me, but when I caught his eye, I waved. I saw his whole face light up when he realised it was me. I loved that about him. It was nice to have someone who seemed genuinely happy to see me.

My dad hadn't noticed any of the exchange. He was scanning the menu. There was quite a big queue. I pointed out that he could use the touchscreens if he wanted but he refused. Apparently, he didn't trust technology. I couldn't use them because they needed a card, and I didn't have one. Yet. It was on my Birthday list, although I didn't reckon I had much of a chance.

Liam carefully tidied up his table. He waved again as he headed to the bins and sorted all his stuff into the right recycling bin. Personally, I wouldn't have bothered. But I knew Liam was different. When he was done, he started a weird series of convoluted gestures which I understood as being him asking if it was ok to come over. I nodded enthusiastically. I wanted it to be crystal clear that he was very welcome to join us.

He pulled his hair across his face so I could only just make out that he was smiling as he came across. When he got close, he reached out and brushed my fingers with his hand. He obviously had no idea who I was with and didn't want to risk fully holding hands. Once more I felt touched by how thoughtful he was. It was quite a stark contrast to the journey in the car with my father.

I smiled at him to reassure him. He flicked his head a little to get the hair out of his eyes, and I saw some sort of shadow on his face. Did he have another bruise? I reached out to move his hair but he pushed my arm away.

"You here on your own Ems?" he asked, sounding hopeful.

"Actually no" and then I continued quickly before he got the wrong idea "I'm here with my dad."

Unlike Lisa, he didn't tell me that I was lying, he just asked me which of the guys was my dad.

"No, hang on, don't tell me. I'll guess" he said with way too much glee in his voice.

He scanned the room. There were a few men around. Some of them had little kids with them. Some of them were on their own. The way I figured it, it boiled down to 3 potential "father" candidates. One in three was pretty good odds.

Eventually Liam point at one of the guys. He was short and bald. I was laughing my head off.

Just then my dad turned and asked me what I wanted. Bit of a giveaway! Having Liam there reminded me of my 'no eating' plan, so I just asked for a mocha.

"Are you allowed coffee?" he asked, surprised.

I looked at Liam and raised my eyebrow. Liam put his hand over his mouth to hide the fact that he was laughing.

"Erm…yes…how old do you think I am?" I snapped. My confidence was obviously boosted by having Liam with me.

"Lose the attitude girl" he snapped back.

Wow. I'd just been told off by my dad. This day sucked. I felt myself welling up. Once more I was a little girl being told off.

Liam stepped in front of me.

"Give her a break" he said.

My dad looked Liam up and down. His hair was hanging over his face, but had shifted slightly so his bruise was more visible. He was wearing his usual scruffy jacket. He smelled nice though. Liam always smelled nice. Clearly, though, my father did not approve.

"Back off pal, I'm having a McDonalds with my daughter." And then he went towards Liam in a threatening manner. Liam flinched and cowered.

"Hey! Leave him alone" I yelled. In fact, I yelled so loudly that everyone in McDonalds went quiet and turned to look at me. I felt my face go bright red. I was sure if you wanted to cook a burger right then, my face would be the perfect place to do it. Then my stomach did a somersault and I felt like I needed the toilet immediately.

"Toilet" I muttered and walked as fast as I could towards the toilets. I went into the stall and sobbed. My dad was going to hate me. Liam was going to hate me. This was the worst day ever.

I took out my phone.

There was a message in WhatsApp. I didn't know if I would have the energy to deal with those guys, but I needed distraction. I didn't want it to be obvious that I'd been crying when I went back out.

Ninja: {{hugs}}

Ninja: Your dad is a bit screwed up eh?

Me: He hates me. He's always hated me but I bet he hates me even more now.

Ninja: Most parents love their kids, no matter how the kid behaves, and no matter how they behave. In fact, if they don't love their kids, they don't love them no matter how they behave. Love and behaviour have nothing to do with each other.

Me: Clearly that's not true.

Caveman: Don't listen to him. You need your dad to love you. It's super duper important. You need to go back out there and let him know you're sorry.

I've got to say, I was more inclined to agree with Caveman. I needed to let my dad know I was sorry. If I left things as they were, he would probably never want to see me again.

Ninja: Remember, he hasn't been in touch for 12 years. This is not about you. You have no power to change this.

That was also a fair point.

Arghh! Why was everything so complicated.

The good news was, everything seemed to have settled a bit now. I'd stopped crying. I was a little bit mad, but not how I'd been before. I did a check of my hair and makeup in the mirror, took a deep breath, and headed back out to face the music.

I looked around. My dad was sat in a booth in the corner. In front of him were three coffee cups. I looked around, and at first I couldn't see Liam anywhere. My heart sank. What had I done?

Then I felt someone grab my hand, it was Liam. He had some packets of sugar and stirring sticks in his other hand. I gave him a big hug. I was so glad to see that he was still there. I couldn't believe how lucky I was.

"Ow!" he winced, as I hugged him.

"Oh god, I'm sorry, did I hug you too tight? It's just I'm so happy you're still here. I thought that you would have given up on me and gone. And I really didn't want you to be upset with me because..."

"Ems...breathe" he chuckled.

He explained what had happened when I had run off to the toilet.

At first her dad had no idea what to do. He'd just stood there. Everybody was looking at him. Liam had seriously considered just leaving, but he wanted to make sure I was alright and couldn't follow me into the toilets without looking really creepy.

So instead Liam had decided to take pity on my dad and help him out. He'd told him what sort of coffee I liked (how did he know that?) and then gone and got a seat. The 3 cups of coffee were for Liam, me and my dad. I'd been gone quite a while so it sounds like they'd had a bit of a chat while I was gone. At first my dad was giving Liam a grilling, but after a while he started talking about himself. It struck me that, at this point, Liam probably knew my father way better than I'd ever done.

He told me how scared my father was about messing up. That's why he was being so weird with me. He felt like he'd messed everything up his whole life, including his relationship with me. That's why he hadn't been in touch before now. Apparently, he was in a new relationship and it had lasted longer than any of his others, so he'd felt ok reaching out to me for the first time.

At this point, there were loads of thoughts racing through my mind. Firstly, how on earth was not being in touch for 12 years better than actually remembering birthdays and stuff? Surely he must realise that made him look way more messed up. Secondly, how on earth did Liam manage to get my dad to open up and tell him so much stuff while I was in the toilet? I was beginning to think Liam was a keeper. If I'd been in his shoes, and threatened in that way, I would have legged it as soon as I had the chance. Especially with the way his dad treated him.

I gave Liam another hug, but gentler this time.

"What was that for?" he asked with a smile on his face.

"Just because." I said, and took his hand and led him to the table where my father was sitting.

My father looked up as I sat down and gestured to one of the coffee cups.

"That's a Mocha. Liam says that's what you like. I hope that's ok." There was a sadness in his eyes that made me feel suddenly very sorry for him.

"Cheers dad."

I forced myself to say dad. For some reason, I felt it was the best thing that I could do in that moment. I was right, his face lit up with a smile that suddenly made him feel so much more familiar. I found myself travelling back in time to a memory of being young girl, sitting next to my dad while he played guitar and I sang. I can't even remember what we were singing. I just remember that we were both giggling.

"Do you still play guitar?" I asked, "Liam plays a bit too don't you Liam?"

Liam looked embarrassed and muttered something about being a bit rubbish at it.

"I'm surprised you remember," smiled my dad, clearly surprised. Then he looked sad again. "I've not played in years. I had to sell all my guitars when I had a bit of a rough patch."

"All of them? That's a shame" I said.

"They are just things" he shrugged, "It's not a big deal. Everything is working out better these days, so I was actually thinking of buying a new one."

There was silence for a moment. I sipped my coffee. It was a bit more bitter than I liked, but it would do for now. My stomach had started rumbling again so the milk in it satisfied my hunger a little.

"Hey, I have an idea" said my dad, "why don't we go get a guitar now? I've been meaning to do it for a while and I'd appreciate your thoughts"

I looked at Liam.

"Liam too" my dad added, "I suspect he will be a little better than you at helping me pick a guitar that plays well." Then he winked at me. I remembered that wink. It made me feel gooey inside.

Well it was certainly a better plan than sitting in McDonalds 'not-eating' for the next couple of hours!

"Sure" I replied, "but bagsy the front seat. Liam can sit in the booster seat in the back." I laughed and punched Liam gently on the shoulder. Instead of joining in and laughing, Liam took a sharp intake of breath and pulled away.

I looked at my dad with my eyebrows raised. My dad looked just as concerned as I felt. There was something going on here and I wasn't sure I was ready to know all the details but I was pretty sure I wasn't going to like it.

"Sorry" I said, reaching out to put my hand on his arm. He flinched again. Then he suddenly stood up and started collecting up the cups. He grabbed his and my dad's and stacked them, and then reached out for mine. Of course, it was still half full. I'm a slow drinker. Even so, I never drink to the bottom. I think this comes from when I used to stay with my granny. She would make afternoon tea every day. She made cakes to go with it. My favourites were these sickly-sweet coconut cakes. They were basically condensed milk and coconut with a glace cherry on top. Actually, now I think about it, they looked just like mini breasts. The thought made me smile. Anyway, she used to make tea in a teapot with actual tealeaves. There was a thing on the wall in the kitchen, and you pressed a button and the tealeaves came out. She'd then pour the tea through a strainer. It was a lovely cuppa. Really milky, just how I like it. But you couldn't drink to the bottom of the cup because if you did you got a mouth full of tealeaves. Since then I'd always left a few centimetres of liquid at the bottom of any hot drink. Add to that the fact that I drank so slowly, it was always cold by the time I got halfway down the cup, then it meant I never finished a drink.

"Sorry" said Liam, "I thought you were done."

"Oh, I am," I explained "I never drink the whole cup of anything."

Now it was Liam's turn to share quizzical glances with my dad.

Liam took the two empty cups and my nearly-full one, and threw them in the appropriate recycling bins, before meeting us outside to head to the car.

My dad led the way and Liam made us both giggle by trying to sit in the booster seat instead of moving it, or sitting on the other side of the car. In the end, he chucked it in the boot and I went and sat on the back seat next to him. My dad joked about feeling like a chauffeur but I could see in the mirror that he was smiling.

We had a good laugh the rest of the afternoon. Dad and Liam were real guitar nerds and at first I felt left out. Then I decided to annoy them by pointing out all the "pretty guitars". The more it annoyed them, the more I did it. At one point they were both jamming away on guitars and everyone in the music shop had stopped to listen to them. I felt quite proud. My dad and my boyfriend. Both words I had barely ever uttered at the start of the week. How quickly things can change!

After a couple of hours in the music shop, loads of guitar solos and endless lengthy conversations with the shop owner about relative merits of the different makes of guitar, my dad walked out of the shop with a new guitar. He and Liam were chattering excitedly and I almost felt forgotten. Weirdly, I didn't mind. I felt a strange sort of contentment. This had been one of the best days that I'd had in a long time. I felt like I fitted in and for those few hours, no one else and nothing else had mattered.

I could tell that once he'd got the guitar, all he wanted to do was go home and play with his new toy.

"I best get you home, it's getting late" he said, glancing at his watch.

I looked at the time on my phone. It wasn't even 5pm yet. Not that late. I had kind of expected him to take us back to his place to show off his guitar, and was a little disappointed that he hadn't offered.

We drove back to my house in relative silence. My dad offered to drop Liam off at his place, but he seemed really reluctant and told my dad not to go out of his way. He said he'd be fine walking from my house.

I was glad about that. I really wanted to talk to him without my dad there.

He pulled up outside of my house. Liam climbed out first and I shuffled over so that I was getting out onto the pavement rather than the road. Once Liam was clear of the car, my dad reached over to my arm.

"Hey Emma," he said "look after that one. He's a keeper"

I nodded. I knew that. I carried on shuffling across. It was kind of awkward because of the cloth on the car seat. Just as I was heading out of the door, he grabbed my arm again.

"And Emma"

"Yeah?" I said impatiently.

"You know I love you don't you? I'm really sorry" he said.

He sounded very genuine.

So why did it upset me so much when he said it? How dare he just throw those words out like that. Love me? Really? He had a really weird way of showing it.

I don't know what he was expecting as a response. Maybe "I love you too daddy". But that's not what he got. I looked away, grunted and closed the car door. I might have slammed it actually. I didn't really mean to slam it. I was just so upset. How dare he!

Liam was standing awkwardly on the pavement, waiting for me. I really wanted to hug him, and kiss him, but I wasn't going to because my father told me I should. How ridiculous was that?

I saw Liam wave to my dad, but by then I was stewing too much to join in. I just grabbed Liam's hand and dragged him up the path with me to my house.

"Is that you Ems?" called my mum as I walked through the door.

"No" I answered sarcastically "It's a burglar coming to nick your coffee supplies"

"Ha ha" A fake laugh was a different response from my mum. Normally she would tell me off for being sarcastic. I could tell, just from those first few seconds, that she was acting differently.

"So how was…" asked my mum, coming out of the kitchen. She stopped when she spotted Liam. "Oh hiya Liam, I didn't know you were here hun."

Hun? That was a bit familiar wasn't it. I could tell my mother liked him. Maybe I'd got it very wrong. I'm sure there is some rule somewhere that says your parents shouldn't like your boyfriend!

Liam said hello. I realised that he didn't know what to call my mother. I'd never told him her name and he couldn't really call her mum. His awkwardness made me smile and forget my annoyance at my dad for a moment.

"I was expecting you home way before now" she continued, "actually" she giggled, "I was expecting you home about 10 minutes after you left! He couldn't even turn up on time again. I figured he'd decide that he had run out time and turn around and bring you straight home. And what was the deal with that unicorn? Pathetic. Then again, what do you expect when he totally ignored you for 12 years…"

My mum went on and on.

I stopped listening. I didn't want to hear her slagging off my dad. She always did this. No matter what he did it was wrong.

"…I hope you haven't had too miserable a time? Ems? Emma? Are you listening to me?"

The next few moments passed in a bit of a blur.

As my mother spoke, I felt an emotion building up inside of me. I wasn't even sure what it was, but it felt like my mum was chipping away at everything that had made today a good day.

"For God's sake mother, give it a rest! No wonder dad never visited before if you always went on at him. In fact, no wonder he left! I've a mind to leave myself right now!"

My mother went quiet. I'd hurt her, I could see. Just as she turned away I saw a tear make its way down her cheek. She brushed it off and took a sudden and intense interest in the kitchen doorway behind her.

"Don't be daft Ems. Where would you go?" she sounded like she was almost pleading.

I didn't think. I just answered "Liam's".

I looked at Liam and there was pure terror on his face.

I didn't mean it. I was just trying to get a rise out of my mother and hurt her for what she was saying. Problem was, I was committed. I couldn't just back off now, it would mean that she had won.

"This is what you always do. You don't care about me. You don't love me. If you did, you wouldn't go on all the time about what a mistake I was, and you would have let my dad come and visit!"

I honestly had no idea what I was saying. I felt totally overwhelmed. All I knew is that I needed to get out of that house. I ignored both of them and stormed out the front door, slamming it behind me. This time I really was trying to make the biggest bang I could.

I walked as fast as I could, in case my mother came after me. It was tricky because I couldn't breathe properly, I was sobbing so much. Everything was so unfair. I automatically turned right towards the shops. Liam's house was in the other direction. In all honestly, I had no intention of staying with him. Frankly, I was scared of his dad (even though I'd never met him).

There was no way I was going to his place. I'd sleep on a bench if I had to, but I was not going home.

I walked until I reached a local park. It was still early and it was a mild enough day. I sat on the bench and replayed the day over and over again.

I could hear my phone pinging away. I didn't want to talk to anyone. It was probably my mum calling me to see where I was. Well, she'd have to stew. Served her right. I lifted my legs up onto the bench and tucked my head into my knees. I was actually feeling a bit dizzy which was not good. At the same time, a part of me was able to appreciate that I could now tuck my legs up like that. Clearly the diet was beginning to work. I could do it before but I couldn't breathe at the same time.

I briefly found it amusing that a part of me could be really upset, and another part could be thinking about successful weight loss.

I let out an involuntary scream and nearly fell off the bench when I felt a hand on my back.

When I looked up my vision was all blurry because I'd been resting my eyes on my knees, so at first I couldn't tell who it was.

"You ok?"

It was Liam. He'd obviously followed me.

I put my face back on my knees. I didn't know what to say.

"You can't come back to mine you know" he said, "I'm really sorry. I didn't want to say in front of your mum though. I didn't think that was fair."

Bless him. He was still being sweet. I didn't want him to feel bad.

I turned to look at him.

"I know." I said "I don't actually want to stay at yours. No offence like."

"None taken" he smiled. "Anything I can do to help?"

I shrugged. I didn't know. I hadn't planned for this. Right now, my only option seemed to be to spend the rest of the night on that bench.

He leaned over, put his hand under my chin, and gently turned my face towards him. He then moved towards me, and kissed me gently on the lips. He let the kiss linger. I didn't make any attempt to break the kiss. It was everything I had wanted it to be. All these years when I'd watched Lisa and others with their boyfriends, I felt left out, like there was something wrong with me. I had yearned to be kissed. At the same time, I was a little scared. What if I was rubbish at it? What if it was gross having someone else's tongue in my mouth and I pulled away and made an idiot of myself?

I imagined what it would be like many times. Nothing had prepared me for the tenderness in this kiss.

When Liam tried to pull away, I wouldn't let him. I turned towards him and looped my arms around his neck. I never wanted that moment to end.

But it did end.

"Gross! What are you two doing?"

It shocked me back into the reality. Stood a few meters away was a kid. He looked about 8-10 years old. His jeans hung around his waist, as if he was too small for them, rather than them being too big for him. Under his arm was a small skateboard. He wore glasses which were sitting crooked on his face.

"Why, do you want some?" I laughed and made out that I was going to move towards him. He screamed and ran away. Liam and I burst into uncontrollable laughter. Just as we wound down the laughter, Liam mimicked the kid screaming and running away and we both lost it again.

It certainly broke the tension in the moment.

"What you gonna do Ems?" Liam asked, once we had calmed down a bit. "You can't come to mine, and you can't stay out here all night."

To be honest, I really didn't know.

"You know" he continued "your mum was really upset when you left. She asked me what she did wrong. She really does care for you. I think she was actually feeling a bit left out because you'd been out with your dad all day. I know what it's like to feel left out. It sucks"

To be honest, I knew too. I hadn't meant what I said. I was just upset after my dad had said he loved me. That hurt so much and yet it shouldn't, should it? Why should I be upset that my dad told me he loved me?

I tried to explain to Liam. He didn't get it.

"I wouldn't know" he shrugged "it's not like my folks care about me. I'm quite jealous of you. At least your mother cares. And your dad seems like a nice guy"

He looked sad. For a moment, I felt like a spoilt, selfish brat. I was just thinking about myself all the time. I saw the way he was around me dad. It was like he was a different guy. My dad seemed to make him feel good about himself, and with a little confidence he seemed to physically hold himself differently.

And yet, I was left with a really strong feeling of betrayal and hurt after today. My mother was the adult here. She shouldn't be jealous of me having a relationship with my dad. Why wasn't she just happy for me? My dad was as bad. I wouldn't have cared about getting toys and stuff off him. I just wanted my dad to love me.

I chuckled to myself. I actually wanted my parents to treat me like a kid. How ironic.

I noticed Liam was glancing at his watch.

"What's up?" I asked.

"I gotta get back." he said "I've got to do my mum's dinner. You gonna be ok? You should come with me and go home. I'll walk you back" he said hopefully.

"Nah. I'm gonna hang here for a while longer." I couldn't go back yet. It was too soon. I needed my mother to realise how upset I was.

Liam shrugged and got up to leave. He paused, turned back to me, leant over and kissed me again. My heart was racing, and yet, at the same time, I felt calmer and more content than I had ever felt in my life.

When the kiss ended, I looked at Liam. He had his scruffy coat on. He hid under his hair, constantly adjusting it to cover more of his face. He was slightly hunched over. And I loved him.

"I love you" I said, and then freaked out. OMG why on earth did I say what I was thinking? When would I learn to keep my mouth shut. I was sure I would never see him again now. Lisa always said you should make boys work for your attention. If you were too full on you would scare them away. Then again, under the circumstances, it might not be advisable to take romance advice from Lisa.

I was so busy panicking, that I didn't hear his reply at first.

"I'm sorry" I said. "It was just the moment, you know…"

"Ems" Liam had sat back down again. "I said I love you too"

He did? He loved me too!

I gave him a huge hug. I could not believe this. He winced again.

"What's up Liam? Why are you wincing?"

"It's nothing" he muttered, looking down at the floor again.

"Liam. You can tell me. It's ok" I gave him a gentle nudge and smiled, "I'm your girlfriend after all"

And then he did tell me. Part of me wished he hadn't. A big part of me. I felt so helpless.

I already knew that his dad could be pretty mean to him and his brother. What I didn't know was that he was also violent.

Last night, Liam had been doing dinner for them all. He couldn't really cook very much because nobody had taught him (I made a mental note to help him with that) so he was just frying some bacon and eggs. His dad had come into the kitchen while he was cooking and asked him about his maths exam. For some reason, Liam had told him that it had not gone well.

Liam shook his head at this point.

"Why am I so stupid?" he asked me. Although he wasn't really talking to me. He was asking himself. I tried to tell him he wasn't stupid but he wasn't listening.

I remembered how Ninja had said you can't time travel, but didn't get the chance to tell Liam because he was telling me the rest of what had happened.

At first his father had just launched in at him for not studying enough, and telling him he was useless like his brother and would never amount to anything. Liam was apparently used to this.

For some reason, on this occasion, he answered back. He said he had been studying.

He stopped the story again. He kept shaking his head and calling himself stupid. I could almost hear his dad's voice. Liam was so not stupid. But right now, it was almost like I didn't exist. He was reliving the whole event.

Anyway, his dad had totally lost it when he answered back, grabbed the pan with the bacon in it and whacked him over it back with it. Hot oil had gone everywhere and even managed to get through his clothes and burn his skin.

It even caught his dad, who then went even more mental at Liam like it was his fault or something. He dragged him physically up the stairs and into his room and locked the door. The bruise on his face wasn't from his dad. Apparently, he made sure he never hit him somewhere it could be seen. The bruise was because his head had caught on the bannister of the stairs while his dad dragged him.

The next morning his dad had gone to his bed to sleep it off. He hadn't remembered locking Liam in, This was something he did quite often apparently, so Liam had taught himself to pick the lock. As soon as he was sure his dad was asleep, he'd left the house and escaped to McDonalds. Which is where we saw him.

It was horrific. It also put everything that was going on with me into perspective.

"You can't go home, Liam" I was pleading with him. How could I sleep knowing anything could happen?

"I have to" he shrugged. "It's always been this way Ems. I'll be fine"

The problem was, it may have always been that way, but I'd not always known about it. I couldn't "un-know" what was going on. I had no idea what to do. What I did know was that I couldn't bear the thought of him going back to his house tonight.

I came up with a crazy plan. He could stay with me. We had a spare room. I'm sure if I told my mother what was going on she'd let him stay. It was perfect.

I told Liam.

He laughed and told me I was sweet but I was being ridiculous.

"Besides, you've kind of run away" he teased.

He had a point. I couldn't leave home and have him come and live with me. I realised I was being stupid and in that moment, I cared way more about Liam than I did about myself.

"Sod it" I said, standing up and gesturing for him to take my hand "Let's go home. I'll tell my mum I'm sorry and you can come and stay with us."

We went home. My mum gave me a huge hug when I walked through the door. From the redness in her face, she must have been crying since I left. I felt bad. I hadn't meant to make her feel that way.

She explained that she had been worried all day because in the past my dad had either not turned up or changed plans last minute and called her to come and fetch me. She'd spent the whole day with her phone waiting for a call. She had all sorts of crazy stories in her head about my dad leaving me somewhere with no money and no working phone. She knew me well enough to know that I often forgot to charge my phone.

By the time I walked through the door she had convinced herself that the worst had happened to me. That's why she reacted the way she did.

I told her about the booster seat in the car and she laughed. I told her about

McDonalds, and Liam and guitar shopping.

We hugged again.

All that time, Liam was standing to the side silently.

I turned to him, took his hand and then finished telling my mother the story of the day.

I gave the short version of what had happened with Liam and his dad. I could feel him shaking while I spoke. He stared at a fix point on the ground, saying nothing the whole time I spoke.

My mother looked as horrified as I was. My mother had always been a sucker for 'lame ducks'. We regularly had friends of hers to stay over for a few nights, because there was something going on in their personal life. She volunteered at a local kids club too, and would often come home and say how much she wished she could take them in and look after them.

She reached over to Liam. He flinched a little but didn't move.

"You can stay here as long as you want, hun."

She then went into mother hen mode. She sorted out the spare room and even dug out some spare clothes and toiletries that he could use. I have no idea where she got them from, but that was a conversation for another day.

Liam said his dad always went down the pub of an evening, so he could probably get his stuff from his house tomorrow night while his dad was out.

"You can stay here as long as you want" said mum "but won't your family notice you are gone? I don't want any trouble"

"Nah" shrugged Liam "my brother disappears for days and no one says a thing."

"Ok, well you're welcome here as long as you want." My mum had her mother hen face on. In that moment, I was so glad she was my mum.

"No sneaking into each other's room in the middle of the night you two!"

My mum laughed as both Liam and I went bright red. Not saying I hadn't thought of it though!

"Muuuum!" I moaned.

When we went to bed, we kissed goodnight. Today was a good day.

SUNDAY: MIND, BODY AND SOUL

I couldn't get out of bed this morning. Well, technically I could, but then I fell over. I was so frustrated. I needed to make sure Liam was ok. I've got the rest of my exams this week too so I really needed to study today.

The clock said 10:14 and I was desperate for the toilet. I would have crawled if it had just been me and mum. She was always up earlier than me on the weekend so I knew she'd be downstairs already. But what if Liam had seen me crawling across the landing? I would have looked like a right Muppet. Problem was, I really did need the toilet so I had no choice.

I tried to walk by holding onto the bed and desk, but my legs kept giving way. In the end, my need to pee outweighed my fear of embarrassment.

There are times where I am absolutely positive that my mother has a webcam set up on the landing. The instant I left my room she yelled upstairs.

"Ems is that you? Are you up now? Liam's already up if you want to come down and get some breakfast"

Dammit. Liam was downstairs. There was no way I could get down the stairs. I would collapse and kill myself. Now if you want to talk embarrassing – the would be incredibly embarrassing.

"Erm…I'm just going to have a bit longer in bed if that's ok. Send Liam up when he's ready"

My mother didn't take too well to the last bit and told me to stop treating her like a slave. It seemed, no matter what I did, I was going to end up being embarrassed.

I just about managed to sit on the toilet. I know, TMI again. But at one point I thought I was going to fall off it. I felt lightheaded and dizzy.

I crawled back to bed, safe in the knowledge that Liam was downstairs. I fell asleep again as soon as my head hit the pillow.

Next time I woke up, the clock said 12:37, and Liam was sat on my bed with a cup of coffee in his hand. I tried to sit up and immediately felt dizzy and light headed again. How is it possible to feel dizzy lying down? I grabbed my head and lay back down.

"You ok?" Liam asked, concerned.

"I'm not sure" I answered "I feel really light headed. It's weird"

Liam went to fetch my mum. When she got upstairs, she sat on the edge of my bed like she had done when I was a little girl. She put her hand on my forehead to check for a temperature and concluded that I didn't have one.

"Do you feel sick?" she asked. I didn't. I didn't feel anything other than weak and lightheaded.

"I bet it's all the stress around exams and stuff" she said.

Why did everyone call everything 'stress'. It was like this catch-all term for anything that was wrong with you:

-Struggling with study. STRESS
-Upset over splitting with a boyfriend. STRESS
-Grumpy because your mum is going on at you. STRESS

What was stress anyway? Seemed to me it was just a way of saying what was wrong with you was all in your head. If you just spend 10 minutes a day going "Om" then you would be fine.

Well this was very real. Whatever 'this' was, I wasn't making it up in my head.

"I'm not stressed" I sighed.

"Well, you have had a lot of pressure these last few weeks. And then yesterday with your dad…" my mother trailed off. I was glaring at her.

"Mum! I am not stressed! I feel light headed when I stand up, or even try and sit up. I feel like someone has drained all the energy from me."

I'd had a good day with my dad yesterday. If anything, I was feeling happier now that I had in a very long time. Whatever was going on here, it was not my fault.

My mum suggested I sleep it off (like that had worked so far) and she and Liam left me in my room.

I decided to Google my symptoms and see if I could work it out. I Google everything. I even Google stuff that my favourite celebrities talk about in their YouTube videos. I am not that fussed when they do the 'how to…' videos, but I love the ones when they talk about their lives. When Zoella talked about her anxiety I really felt like she was describing me and my life. It was a bit disappointing when she said she would probably have to live with it for the rest of her life, but at least she had got to a place where she could do more stuff.

Maybe she needed Liam's breathing thing? I should message her and let her know. Although she'd probably ignore someone like me.

I went to her channel and looked to see if she'd ever had anything like this. I didn't find anything but I did re-watch a few of her videos about anxiety. I posted a comment with Liam's breathing technique. I didn't expect her to read it, but maybe it would help some of her other followers.

It sounds ridiculous, but even typing was a huge effort. I decided to take my mother's advice and get some more sleep.

When I woke up again it was gone 6pm. I had spent the whole day sleeping. My mum was stood there with a hot drink in her hand, that smelled like coffee. It must have been her that woke me up.

"How are you doing love?" she asked with concern.

I tried to sit up and immediately felt weak and lay back down.

"Awful" I groaned.

I looked around my mother to see if Liam was there but couldn't see him.

"He's gone to get his stuff" my mum said, guessing what I was looking for. "Can you sit up? You need to get something to eat and drink"

The last thing I needed right now was my mother force feeding me. I told her there was no way I could sit up. It was only half a lie. I probably could have managed it if I really wanted to, but I didn't.

"Right," she said, standing up "I'm going to get you something you can drink with a straw. Maybe a milkshake or something. If you're no better tomorrow you need to get to the doctors. What exams do you have this week?"

I groaned. Oh god, exams. Of course. I have the rest of them this week. Luckily it's Art tomorrow and I don't need to do anything for that. I told my mother and she nodded and left my room.

I wiggled myself more into an upright position, trying not to make any sudden moves, and grabbed my phone. I thought I'd message Lisa and check if she was ok. Maybe it was a virus or something. Besides, I wanted to see how she was getting on. It felt like forever since I'd last caught up with her.

There was a WhatsApp message waiting for me.

Caveman: You're mean. I'm starving. We're going to die *sob*

What was his problem now?

Ninja: Ignore him. He's like you, he's grumpy when he's hungry.

Me: I am not grumpy when I'm hungry! And anyway, I'm not hungry. Far from it. My stomach isn't rumbling at all and I can't face the thought of food.

Ninja: That's because your stomach has shrunk. Your body is now eating into muscle to get the energy it needs. Google it. I bet the it comes up with the symptoms you are experiencing now.

I Googled it. Only because I wanted to prove him wrong. I would know if I was hungry:

Dehydration – I was thirsty all the time lately. So much so, I'd even started drinking water which is unheard of for me. I hate water. It tastes of nothing. I've never really had enough to drink. When I was little I ended up in hospital I was so dehydrated. After much nagging I started drinking Coke. I always had a bottle with me to try and force myself to drink more. But there is so much sugar in Coke, I'm sure that is one of the reasons that I am so fat. So I tried to drink less, but then I wasn't really drinking anything. I was constantly thirsty so I had to switch to water.

Decreased Resting Metabolic Rate – From Biology (and what Caveman has said before) this is about how you process your food. I've always thought my Metabolism is screwed up. If I even look at a packet of crisps I put weight on, but Lisa seems to be able to eat anything she wants. Oh God, what if I was making my Metabolic rate even worse? Breathing in the fumes of the chips must have been making me put weight on!

Loss Of Monthly Menstrual Periods – I thought back to when my last period was. I was never very regular so I didn't particularly keep track of when I was next due. But when I thought about it, it was at least 7 weeks since my last period. That wasn't normal. If I'd been having sex, I'd have been panicking that I was pregnant by now.

Fatigue -Well that summed up what I was feeling right now pretty well. Bugger.

High Blood Pressure – I think problems with blood pressure can lead to dizziness can't they? Double bugger.

I think Caveman might be right. This certainly ticked all the boxes for starvation. But how can that be true? I've been eating. Yesterday…well yesterday I didn't eat anything but the day before I did. I had a couple of chips. Oh. As I thought through the last couple of weeks I hadn't eaten.

Bugger. Caveman was right. I was starving.

What was I going to do? If I start eating I am going to turn into a giant whale and Liam will never want to see me again and I'll never get another boyfriend. It's taken me forever to get this one.

ping

Ninja: Liam doesn't care. I've told you before. He loves you for who you are not how you look.

I didn't believe him. All those celebrities I see are always changing their image. There are no famous fat people that everyone looks up to. Even those fat celebrities that say they are fine with their size lose loads of weight, like Adele or Amy Schumer. Weight matters. Looks matter.

The problem was, they were both right. It looks like the reason for my current weakness and dizziness was a lack of food. I had no idea what to do. I couldn't tell my mum, she'd go mental and force feed me. She'd done that before where she watched everything I ate and forced me to have breakfast and stuff. I'd had to get really creative to fool her. I even made myself sick when I got to school. Eventually I managed to fool her into thinking I was back to normal and she stopped watching.

I bet the doctor would work it out straight away. My mum would come in with me too and then she would go mental at me when the doctor told her what was going on.

Somehow, I needed to get enough energy to stop my mum taking me to the doctors tomorrow (and to revise for exams) but not eat so much that I turned into a beached whale, again.

I put my phone down and cried. I felt so desperate and hopeless. I closed my eyes and lay in bed with the tears running down my face and making my pillow soggy. I didn't care. Every time I felt calmer, I thought of how unfair everything was and how I was going to end up old and fat and lonely, and the tears started again.

I heard someone coming up the stairs and frantically wiped my tears away. I couldn't let me mother see me like this. I rolled over on my side and pretended to be asleep.

I heard the door open. I feigned breathing steadily. Then I heard a whispered conversation and I realised Liam was back. I may not have wanted to talk to my mother, but I did want to talk to Liam.

I moaned and moved, as if they had woken me up with their whispers.

Liam came over and sat on the edge of the bed. He had a milkshake in his hand. Banana, my favourite. It was in my special unicorn bottle that I'd had since I was younger. He gestured for me to take it, and I struggled and sat up in bed and took it off him. This seemed to make my mum happy, and she turned around and left us both alone in the room. Although she left the door open, obviously. It amused me. I had no idea what she thought I could get up to in this state.

Liam was flushed. His hair was even more messy than usual and there was sweat pouring down the sides of his face. As he held out the milkshake to me, I could see his hands were shaking.

I took the bottle off him, not to drink, but to allow him to have his hand back. He tucked it into his jacket pocket as soon as I took the milkshake off him.

"How'd you get on?" I asked, pretending like I hadn't guessed.

He shrugged and stared at a fixed spot on my carpet. I thought he was going to cry. He didn't speak for a minute or so.

"Erm…well, I got my stuff" he said, "but as I was coming out my dad arrived back.I don't know what he was doing there. He'd normally be down the pub all evening. I don't think he would have said anything, but he noticed I had a holdall as well as my rucksack." He stopped again and swallowed hard, and continued.

"He grabbed my arm and asked if I'd been home last night. I didn't know what to say. He obviously didn't know if he was asking. But he was holding my arm so tight, it really hurt. I couldn't think. I didn't say anything and that annoyed him more"

I saw Liam flinch as he thought about what happened. I wanted to be able to tell him it was ok, that he didn't have to tell me, but I wanted to know. I wanted to comfort him, stroke his face, hold his hand. But his hands were in his pocket and his face was pouring with sweat, or maybe tears.

"He erm…he punched me on the back of my head hard and told me to answer him. I didn't know what to do so I tried to pull away. That just made him hold me tighter." Liam rubbed his arm unconsciously. I could see a scared little boy, trying to be brave.

"He shook me, and when I tried to pull away, I went flying onto the ground. Luckily my head landed on my holdall, but my shoulder hit the path hard. When I tried to get up, he kicked me back down again. He told me I was more useless than my brother and just taking up space. He said I should just disappear and never come back. Then he walked into the house, so I left".

I didn't know what to say.

"Did you tell mum what had happened?" I asked.

He shook his head.

"You should. You might need to go to A&E"

He shook his head again.

"I've had worse" he said, "I'll be fine." Then he smiled "At least he won't have a problem with me staying her now".

He sniggered, and then he groaned. He was clearly hurt quite badly.

"I really wish you'd get checked out" I said, concerned.

"Oh like you have done for this?" he said, waving his hand over me.

He was changing the subject, and I knew it. I felt bad. Here was me, with a self-inflicted problem, and here he was taking a genuine interest in me just after his father had beat him up.

I don't know whether it was guilt, or feeling sorry for him, or just needing someone to talk to, but I found myself telling him how I was feeling and why.

I told him about Googling my symptoms and what it had said. I told him about not eating. I told him about feeling fat and ugly compared to everyone else. I told him that I was worried that he wouldn't like me anymore if I started eating. I burst into tears when I told him my metabolism was screwed up and so whatever I ate would make me the size of a beached whale.

I expected him to get up and leave the room. After everything he had to put up with, I must have seemed so pathetic.

He didn't. He leaned over (wincing as he moved) and gently kissed me.

"Drink the milkshake you Muppet" he said, pushing the bottle in my hand closer to my mouth.

"Do you know how long I've fancied you for?" he asked.

The question caught me by surprise. Despite the way he was with me, I didn't really think that he fancied me. I also thought this had only started this week because of the whole photo on the bus thing.

"Erm..5/6 days?" I asked.

"I've fancied you since primary school" he laughed.

What? Was he serious? I was a chubby kid in primary school. How could he possibly have fancied me then?

"Stop trying to be nice" I said, "there is no way you even noticed me at primary school, let alone fancied me."

As I said that, I realised that I remembered him from Primary school. I may not have fancied him, but I'd always been aware of him. Maybe he wasn't lying?

"I'm serious Ems. You always made me laugh. And all the other kids! And while we were all tiptoeing around the teacher, trying not to get told off, you seemed to be having a right laugh. I always wished you'd talk to me, but you never seemed to see me. You were always joking around with your friends. I even tried to talk to you once but you totally blanked me. I was upset for days. I felt like a right Muppet for even trying. "

Talk about a guilt trip. I didn't remember him talking to me. Clearly, he wasn't lying about fancying. He even remembered me clowning around.

"But how could you fancy me? I was the chubby kid. Other girls were so much prettier. Lucy was gorgeous and all the boys loved her."

Lucy was what I would call 'classically beautiful'. She was like a princess with long blond hair that was always immaculately tied up. Her clothes were always so neat and tidy. I hated brushing my hair so my hair was always a bit scruffy. I always spilled my food down my top so even my clothes were scruffy. She was brilliant at all sport too. On school sports day, she would leave everyone in her dust. She never got in trouble

"Boys were scared of Lucy. I know I was. She was so up herself. She may have looked pretty, but she wasn't a very nice person."

He had a point. I so wanted to be like Lucy, or at least friends with her, but I was invisible to her. When I was 9 she moved away and I got to be friends with all her friends. That was a great day. Her friends told me all these bizarre stories about the things they were and weren't allowed to do around her. She was apparently very controlling. She also banned her friends from having certain hairstyles and wearing certain clothes because she was really insecure about her looks, and hated being upstaged by anyone else.

The weirdest thing was when one of her friends, Samantha, said that she was jealous of me. Me! How on earth could anyone be jealous of me? Especially someone who was as together as Lucy. When I asked why, they said it was because I was so funny. All the boys wanted to hang out with me. I wish I'd known at the time. I thought nobody liked me.

I guess, now I think of it, I could see why Liam would like me more than Lucy. But then, kids didn't care as much about looks at that age.

"Ok, so why do you still fancy me now? There are way more good looking girls in high school. You can have your pick."

Liam laughed.

"Seriously Ems, you crack me up. Who would want to be with me?"

"I would" I replied. I felt guilty though. Because I hadn't given him a second glance until this week. In fact, I'd always looked down on him.

"Besides," he continued "what makes you think I'm scraping the bottle of the barrel with you? Who do you reckon I should fancy more than you?"

I thought about it. My first thought was to say Lisa. She seemed to constantly have the attention of the boys, but when I thought about what went on with Stu, I could see why. I wouldn't want to be like Lisa.

The more I thought about it, the more I realised that I couldn't think of anyone who's name I would suggest to Liam.

"See? You are great Ems. You are funny and down to earth. You don't play stupid games and you are genuinely a nice person. Why would I want to be with anyone else?"

ping

This was all proving a bit much to process. I checked my phone because I really didn't know what to say to Liam. I did know I had a warm fuzzy feeling inside right now.

Ninja: Told you so

Caveman: Can we eat now?

I laughed out loud. I didn't mean to. Liam looked put out and asked who I was talking to.

It struck me that now, while we were being so honest with each other, might be the best time to tell him about my WhatsApp friends. Then again, that might be the thing that tipped him over the edge and sent him away.

"You don't have to tell me," he said snottily "if it's private."

He always seemed to get a bit agitated when I was on my phone. Maybe it was because he didn't have one himself. Or maybe it was because he assumed that I was talking about him. Which I was of course, but not in the way he thought.

"Ok, so this might seem a bit weird" I suggested "but erm..well...you see...since the start of the week, I've been messaging with a couple of guys on WhatsApp."

"I knew you were talking to other guys." Liam was sulking now.

"No, not like that. Honestly. This is way worse...I mean weirder." Oh god, I had no idea how to explain this.

"You know how sometimes you have different voices in your head telling you different stuff?" I asked.

"Like what?" said Liam. He was looking confused but at least now he was listening.

"Well, maybe a part of you wanted to come over and talk to me, but another part of you was really scared that you would get ignored like when you were younger."

Liam nodded.

"Ok, well my parts are on WhatsApp." I looked at him expectantly. "And they send me messages." I added for good measure. Might as well get it all out there now I'd started.

"Like what? What was that they just said" he asked. I don't think he believed a word of what I was saying, but at least he hadn't legged it yet!

I showed him my phone.

"What does he mean by 'told you so'?" Liam asked.

"Well, Ninja said you loved me for who I was and didn't care how I looked. Oh and Caveman thinks everything is going to kill me so he was sulking at me because he said I was starving. Although funnily," I laughed a little nervous laugh, "it turns out he might have been right."

Liam was reading the other messages. At first I wanted to snatch my phone off him. It felt like I should keep them private somehow. But I resisted. I wanted everything to be open. As he read he began to nod. Occasionally he sniggered.

After he'd finished, he looked at me.

"They're right. I don't want you to be anything other than you are. And this not eating thing is crazy. It's making you ill. At this rate, you aren't even going to be able to do your exams. We need to get your mum to do you some food."

Oh my god, he was going to tell my mum.

"You can't tell my mum. Promise me? She'll go spare at me and start watching all my meals again."

"Again?" he asked "have you done this before?"

I genuinely felt embarrassed. It seemed so silly now to make myself ill by not eating.

"Just promise me Liam. I beg you."

He leaned over and kissed me again, just as my mum walked in the room.

She raised her eyebrows.

"Promise you what?" she asked.

Liam looked at me and winked.

"She said to promise I'd go out and buy her a bag of chips for her dinner" he said.

"Oh Ems, you should probably have something healthier than that if you've been ill." My mother had gone into full on mothering mode.

"I'm feeling better, mum" I lied. I wasn't. But I did want chips for my dinner and I figured that was the only way I was going to get them.

"It's ok" said Liam "I'll go get and get them for her. Do you want some?"

My mum immediately grabbed her tummy and said that she shouldn't. And I wondered why I was so self-conscious?

"Go on" said Liam in full charm mode "I won't tell anyone. And it will be setting a good example to Emma. I think she could do with the energy for her studying."

I panicked for a moment. I thought he was going to tell her why I was ill. But he cleverly managed to imply it without actually saying it.

"Well I suppose it won't matter too much this once." She smiled.

Liam got up and gave me a kiss on my forehead.

"Drink the milkshake, it will help" he whispered while he was close.

"Give me a tick and I'll go and sort out some money for you" my mum said, heading out of the door.

"Oh no, it's ok. I have plenty" Liam said before she got out of the room.

"Well that may have been true before but your living here now" she said, "your money will run out quickly if you keep buying us dinner".

"Don't worry" Liam replied "My dad gives me money every month. I think it's so he can believe he's a good dad and totally ignore me."

Ok, now it was my turn to be confused. I thought Liam's dad was the violent pig that lived up the road. He didn't strike me as the sort of person that would give Liam money.

Liam clearly read my mind.

"Oh no, not him. That's actually my Stepdad. It's my real dad that gives me the money. I never see him. He just gives me money."

It occurred to me that I knew very little about Liam. I looked forward to learning more about him in the future.

For now, I was just happy to have found someone who seemed to genuinely like me, and who I could talk to about anything.

When Liam left, I did as I was told. I drank the milkshake. When it first hit my stomach, I felt really sick and I thought of pouring it down the bathroom sink and pretending I'd had it. But I didn't want to let Liam down, so I slowly sipped away until it was all gone.

When I reached the end, my stomach rumbled. I took that as a good sign.

By the time Liam returned from the chippy, I was well enough to head downstairs and eat it there. It was a nice feeling, the three of us, sitting around, eating chips and arguing over what to watch on Netflix.

For the first time in as long as I could remember, I felt contended.

This did strike me as a little crazy given I had exams coming up, had been feeling rubbish all day because I'd been starving myself, had seen my dad for the first time in 12 years, had fallen out with my best friend, and had gained a boyfriend who had to leave home because his dad was beating him up!

Phew! What a week!

ABOUT THE AUTHOR

Dawn C. Walton was born in North Wales in 1972. She is now a happily married mother of one girl and is a full-time Cognitive Hypnotherapist with her own practice in Dundee, Scotland.

Printed in Great Britain
by Amazon

35835955R00087